Contents

1 Europe and the world in 1918

Introduction

▶ *Why did world peace after 1918 last only to 1939?*

International relations are the history of how countries deal with each other. For example they may make alliances to protect themselves against other countries. International relations involves a great deal of talking. If countries stop talking and relations between them break down they may resort to war. This is what happened before the First World War.

This book begins and ends with photographs of suffering and destruction caused by war. The first photograph (Source **A**) shows some of the sailors wounded in the First World War, in which 20 million people died. The photograph on page 94 (Source **F**) was taken during the Second World War, in which another 37 million people were to die. The twenty or so years that passed between these two photographs were taken up with international attempts to establish a lasting peace in Europe. These attempts failed, but many lessons can be learnt from this failure. Perhaps some of the lessons have been learnt as we have not yet had another world war, although historians may argue we have come very close to it.

There were three key events before 1920 which had a great effect on International Relations up to the Second World War. These were:

1 The First World War 1914–18.
2 The Russian Revolution in 1917.
3 The Peace Treaties 1919–20.

We want you to ask the type of questions that a historian asks. For example, what were the causes of the Second World War? Source **B** shows that these three events caused problems which in turn helped cause another war. Historians ask questions such as: Why and how did this happen? Which were the most important causes of war? This book will help you answer such questions.

First the book looks at these three key events. Then it examines the attempts to keep international peace. After the First World War people wanted to find a new way to keep international peace so the League of Nations was set up. But the League's supporters faced major problems including:

1 The failure of the USA to join the League.
2 The World Economic Depression.
3 The rise of new political ideas such as fascism in Italy, Germany and Spain and aggressive nationalism in Japan.

Source A Wounded British Sailors after the battle of Jutland, 1916

```
                                      Peace
                                      Treaties
              WAR

  1914              1917  1918  1919  1920        1922

                    Revolution  US                Mussolini
                    in Russia   isolation         comes to
                    p.6         begins            power
                                p.38              in Italy
                                                  p.44

         WILSON            LLOYD     CLEMENCEAU   MUSSOLINI
                           GEORGE
```

Source B Events leading up to the Second World War

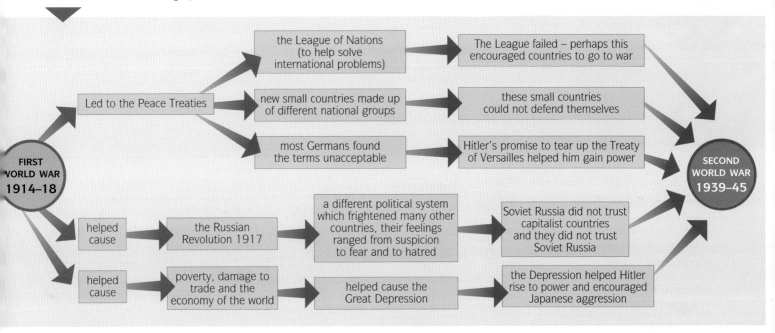

By the mid 1930s the League was failing to keep international peace and Europe was again beginning to split into two armed camps and war was a possibility. In 1939 the Second World War began in Europe, by 1941 it was a world war. The major events and developments are shown on the timeline (Source **C**). The timeline includes page numbers to help you find a topic. You will see that many of the topics and events overlap, for example the work of the League of Nations overlaps with the collapse of international peace and the rise of the Nazi Party in Germany. This is because these events and developments affect each other, for example the World Depression is a key reason for Hitler coming to power. You could ask the following questions: Would the Second World War have happened without Hitler coming to power? Would Hitler have come to power without the World Depression? Would the Depression have happened without the First World War and the Peace Treaties? The answer is almost certainly no!

Source C

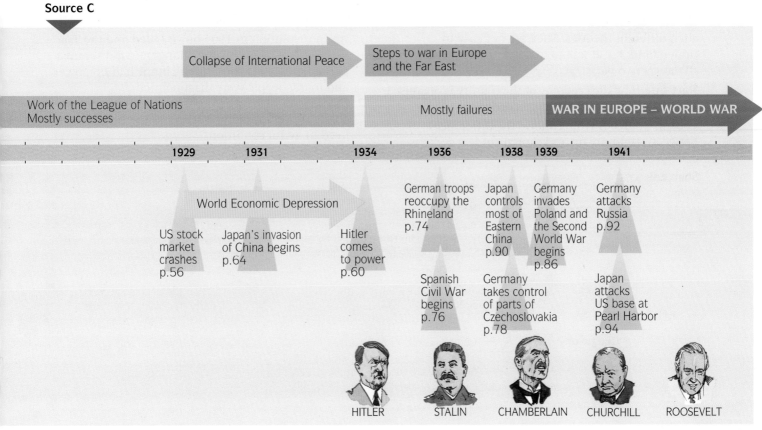

Revolution in Russia

▶ ## Why did the world fear Communism?

What do you fear or hate most? Snakes? School? You probably would not say 'ideas', yet many people fear or hate other people's ideas and beliefs. Winston Churchill, a member of the British Government in 1919, feared communist ideas and beliefs more than anything.

Source A Winston Churchill

▼

Communism is not a policy, it is a disease. Communism means war of the most ruthless character, the slaughter of men, women and children, the burning of homes, and the inviting of tyranny, disease, and famine…

In 1917, before the end of the First World War, there was a Communist Revolution in Russia.

What is communism?

There are different theories about how countries should be run. Communism and capitalism are two such different theories. They are not easy to understand, but it will help if you think of each theory as two parts:

Part one How the economy of the country is organised.
Part two How politics is organised.

Look at Source **B** which shows the differences between communism and capitalism.

The world in 1916 was capitalist. Yet communists believed in world revolution, therefore, communism was feared by most of the leaders of the capitalist countries such as Britain, France and the USA. When a powerful country such as Russia became communist it was bound to have a great effect on international relations. To understand the effects it is helpful to take a brief look at why and how the revolution in Russia happened.

Why was there a revolution?

Compare Sources **C** and **D**. They show the extremes of rich and poor in Russia. Of the 125 million Russians very few were as rich as the people in Source **C**. Most Russians were peasants who worked and lived in dreadful conditions. They regularly suffered from famine and starvation. The extremes of rich and poor is one reason why there was a revolution in Russia. The other reasons are:

1 Russia was ruled by the Tsar Nicholas II who had absolute power. Many Russians resented this and wanted a say in how Russia was governed. There was a revolution in 1905 but it failed and the Tsar kept control by promising change. He did set up a parliament called the 'Duma', but it had no power and many people were disappointed.
2 Russia was a backward country but industry was changing very rapidly. Workers in the new factories lived in awful conditions.

Source B ▶

	Communism	Capitalism
Economics	Workers create wealth, so factories, mines, banks and other means of production should be owned by the State for the benefit of the workers and people.	Businesses and land are owned not by the State but by individuals – often through owning shares in a company. Profits go to the owners of the business.
Politics	The Communist Party is the only political party allowed. The people rule themselves through the party.	Every so often the people choose the political party they want to run the country by voting them into power.
Geography	Communism is international: Communists should work for a world revolution by encouraging revolution in other countries.	Capitalism aims for a strong nation state.

Source C Dinner at a ball for the rich in St Petersburg in 1914

Source D Dinner at a soup kitchen for the unemployed in pre-war St Petersburg

3 The First World War was a disaster for Russia. The price of food shot up because of shortages. There were many defeats for the army.

4 People were unhappy with the influence that a religious man called Rasputin had on the Tsar's wife, the Tsarina.

How did the revolution happen?

By 1917 many Russians were ready for another revolution. In fact there were two revolutions. First in March 1917 there were strikes and riots in St Petersburg. Soldiers and sailors joined the strikes and law and order broke down. The Tsar was forced to abdicate. The Duma set up a Provisional Government to run Russia, but the workers and soldiers in Petrograd did not accept this and set up 'soviets' (councils) to run things in the city. Among the revolutionaries was a group of communists led by Lenin. This struggle continued until November 1917 when the second revolution happened and the communists in the soviets defeated the Provisional Government. Lenin set up a Communist Government and ended the war against Germany. In 1923 Russia was renamed the USSR (Union of Soviet Socialist Republics).

Questions

1 Which communist ideas would most people in Source **C** fear? Who in Source **C** might not fear such ideas?

2 Explain why the people in Source **D** might be attracted by communist ideas?

3 Draw a cartoon strip with six pictures showing the following events of the Russian Revolution: defeats in the war; the strikes of March 1917; the Tsar abdicates; the Provisional government and soviets; the second revolution of March 1917; the end of the war with Germany.

4 What earlier event suggests that if Russia had not been involved in the First World War there would not have been a revolution in 1917?

New ideas and old ideas

 What were the types of political movement emerging in post-war Europe?

Study Source **A**, it shows that communism was not the only new political idea which appeared in Europe around this time.

Source A

1917	The Communist Revolution in Russia.
1919	The Comintern (the Communist International) set up to encourage revolutions in other countries.
1919	Communist revolutions in Germany and Hungary fail.
1922	Fascists led by Benito Mussolini seize power in Italy.
1932	A fascist government takes control in Portugal.
1936–39	The Civil War in Spain is won by general Franco and his fascist party.

The other new idea was fascism. There were also other types of government, many countries were increasingly more democratic and believed the leader should be elected by the people. Some countries were republics and others were monarchies. To help you make sense of all these names study Source **B**.

Source B

Type of State	Head of State	Examples	Democratic?
Monarchy	King, Queen, Tsar or Emperor	Britain, Italy, Russia before 1917. Germany before 1919. Austria-Hungary before 1919. Spain until 1931. China until 1911. Japan.	Britain was democratic, the others were not.
Republic	President	USA, France, Germany 1919–34. Spain 1931–39.	Yes
Dictatorship	Dictator	Italy after 1922. Russia after 1924. Germany after 1934. Spain after 1939.	No

You can see from Source **B** that some countries changed. For example Germany and Spain were first monarchies, later republics and then dictatorships. But the picture is really more complicated as the following points show:

1. Britain, although a monarchy, was also increasingly democratic. All men and later women voted to choose the government.
2. In 1922 Mussolini became dictator of Italy but the King continued to be the head of state, although he had no real power.
3. Japan had an Emperor but many historians believe the country was run by big companies and the army.
4. Russia was a communist state but when Stalin came to power he ruled Russia as a dictator.

Source C Governments in Europe in 1936

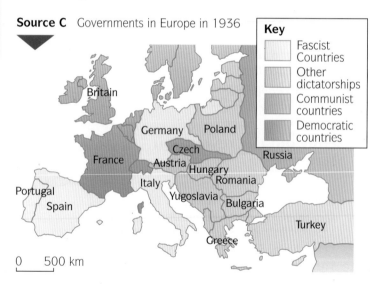

Key
- Fascist Countries
- Other dictatorships
- Communist countries
- Democratic countries

0   500 km

The range of views and the features of the different types of governments are show in Source **D**.

The 'political spectrum'

Communism and fascism are very different in their aims but are very similar in their methods of controlling a country. Fascism glorifies the nation state – people have to serve the state. Whereas communism is international and aims at the end of the nation state so that workers can rule the world. In practise, the way that communism and fascism control the lives of the people is very similar, they are both totalitarian.

Source D

DEMOCRACY

Features

1 Personal freedoms e.g. to vote and say what one believes.
2 More freedom for the media, trade unions, clubs, youth movements and churches.

LEFT WING	CENTRE	RIGHT WING
PARTIES		
Communist	Socialists, Liberal/Social Democrats	Conservatives Fascist

USSR (Russia)
China after 1949

← Britain →
← USA →
← France →
Depending on which party is elected

Italy, Spain, Nazi Germany. (Facism differed in Germany, Italy and Spain. Nazism was more totalitarian, more brutal and more racist.)

COMMUNISM

Features

1 Obedience to a strong leader.
2 No opposition parties allowed.
3 Many personal freedoms not allowed – totalitarian.
4 A large army.
5 The state owns the means of production (e.g. industry, agriculture, transport, banks).

Methods

TOTALITARIANISM

Total control over every aspect of people's lives, including what people believe and say. The following are strictly controlled: the press, the media, the Church, clubs and societies, trade unions, education, youth movements, entertainment.

FASCISM

Features

1 Obedience to a strong leader.
2 No opposition parties allowed.
3 Nationalism (a strong desire to make one's country more powerful).
4 A belief that one's race is superior to others.
5 Many personal freedoms not allowed – totalitarian.
6 A large army.
7 Hatred of communism.
8 The State controls the means of production and uses it to make the nation strong.
9 Violence to be used, if necessary, to achieve fascist aims.

 Questions

1 Which countries were most likely to make alliances with Mussolini's Italy?

2 Which countries were most unlikely to make an alliance with communist Russia?

3 For each of the following quotations decide what the political belief of the person who said it was (democratic, communist or fascist).

a) 'One State, One Leader, One People.'

b) 'Let the ruling classes tremble at a... revolution. In it the proletarians (workers) have nothing to lose but their chains. They have a world to win. Working men of all countries unite.'

c) 'We look forward to a world founded upon four essential human freedoms. The first is freedom of speech and expression – everywhere in the world. The second is freedom of every person to worship God in his own way... The third is freedom from want... The fourth is freedom from fear...'

Solving the causes of the war

▶ *How would you solve the problems which caused the war?*

The war had been caused by a number of long-term problems between the Great Powers in Europe. How would you prevent these problems causing another war? In 1914 the powerful countries in Europe were divided into two alliances.

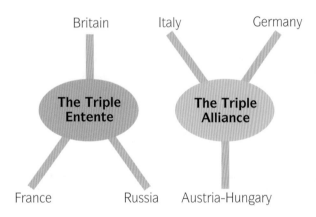

Britain   Italy   Germany

The Triple Entente   **The Triple Alliance**

France   Russia   Austria-Hungary

The immediate problem which caused the war was the murder of the heir to the throne of Austria-Hungary, Archduke Franz Ferdinand. He was killed by a Serb called Gavrillo Princip. Austria-Hungary and Serbia were enemies and the murder gave Austria-Hungary an excuse to attack Serbia. Serbia, however, was supported by Russia. Austria-Hungary and Russia were in different alliances. So when they went to war the other members of the alliances quickly became involved.

The reason the countries of the Triple Alliance and Triple Entente were prepared to go to war was not the murder of the Archduke but the long-term problems between them. These problems are shown opposite. For each problem suggest how it could be avoided in the future. Forget for the moment that Germany lost the war and try to be fair to both sides. Your teacher may want you to discuss this task in pairs or groups and come to a joint decision, after all, international relations involves much discussion. Later in the book you can find out if any of your ideas were tried out.

Problems behind the Great War

Problem 1 – The rise of Germany

In the 1860s Germany was not one country but separate states. The most powerful was Prussia which wanted to unite the German States. In 1870–71 France went to war with Prussia to stop her uniting Germany. Prussia won. Once united, Germany's economy grew rapidly. Her industrial strength overtook that of Britain, only that of the USA remained stronger. In 1888 Kaiser Wilhelm became the new ruler of Germany. He wanted Germany to be more successful by being more aggressive towards other countries. Therefore, Germany used her economic wealth to build up a very powerful army and navy. Other countries in Europe were worried by Germany's strength.

Problem 2 – The Arms Race

The growing power of Germany's army and navy meant that other countries tried to match them and so an arms race developed. In particular Britain began in 1906 to build new, more powerful ships called 'Dreadnoughts'. Germany did the same. The French increased their army to four million soldiers and the Russians spent heavily on building railways to move their troops quickly to their borders with Germany and Austria-Hungary.

Problem 3 – Problems in the Austro-Hungarian Empire

Germany's ally, Austria-Hungary, was in trouble. It was struggling to control parts of its empire in the Balkans, this included Bosnia (see Source **A**). Some Balkan countries such as Serbia were independent. Many people in Bosnia were Serbs and wanted to be ruled by Serbia. Austria-Hungary wanted to defeat Serbia in a war to end this threat.

The European powers believed that to be great you needed an overseas empire. Germany was only united in 1871, long after other European powers, such as Britain and France, had created empires. So there were few territories left for Germany. Kaiser Wilhelm believed that now Germany was rich and strong she also should have an empire. In 1905 and 1911 the Kaiser tried to force Britain and France to allow Germany to expand its empire in Africa. He failed but the tension and fears between the European powers increased.

In 1879 Germany signed an alliance with Austria-Hungary. In 1882 Italy joined. This was known as the Triple Alliance. France and Russia feared Germany and in 1892 signed an alliance. By 1907 Britain had sided with France and Russia in the Triple Entente. Europe was now divided into two armed camps. All it needed was a spark to start a dispute between the two sides.

The Spark!

On 28 June 1914 a Serb shot the heir to the throne of Austria-Hungary. The countries of the two alliances were quickly involved and Europe was at war.

Source A Europe in 1914

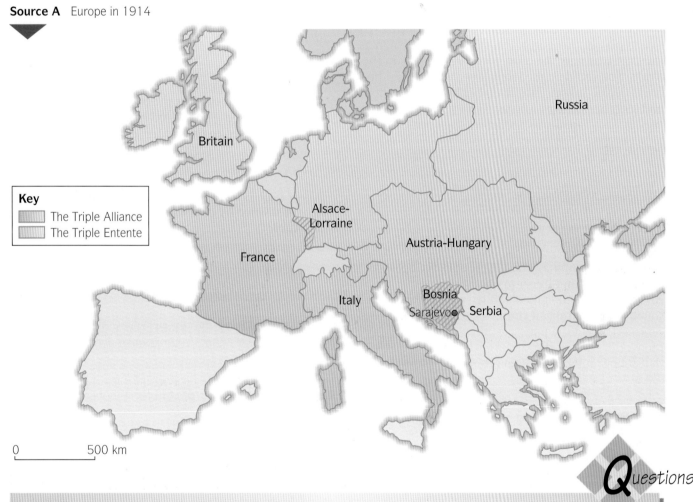

Key
- The Triple Alliance
- The Triple Entente

0   500 km

Questions

1 Consider Problem 1 on page 10. Try to solve the problem of Germany being too strong and aggressive. How do you suggest this problem is controlled or removed?

2 Look at Problem 2. How would you solve the problem of a Europe armed to the teeth. After all, if you believe your armed forces are strong you may be more tempted to use them.

3 Decide what can be done about Problem 3. Good luck, the different national groups in this area of Europe are still fighting and arguing today.

4 What can you do to solve Problem 4 and grant Germany's wish for an empire? Is it possible to keep all the Great Powers happy?

5 Problem 5 is a very dangerous situation. How would you prevent a new alliance system after the war?

The world outside Europe

 What problems were there outside Europe?
Which countries were the rising powers?

There were plenty of problems troubling international relations in Europe, but there were also plenty of problems in the rest of the world. The First World War had been fought mainly in Europe. The Second World War was to be fought in many continents. By 1919 there were nations outside of Europe which were strong enough to be called Great Powers. The most powerful was the USA which now had to decide what role to play in the world. This was a vital decision as the USA was now the most powerful country in the world. She could be the world's peacemaker or she could decide to concentrate on her problems at home and let other nations solve their own squabbles. In the Far East Japan was the growing power. Other problems included the two troubled giants of Russia and China, Britain's Empire which was the largest in the world and the ambitions of Italy which wanted to enlarge its Empire.

The USA

The USA did not agree that European powers should control large empires. The USA fought for democracy and the rights and freedoms of small nations. Many Americans were horrified and fed up with the squabbles of European countries and their empires.

America had the power to act as peacemaker for the world. Look at the status of the other countries that follow and decide if you think she wanted to do so.

The British Empire

Britain's problem was protecting its world-wide Empire. In the 1920s and 30s it would struggle to do this.

Russia (USSR)

Russia was a huge country with huge potential. The civil war in Russia was over by 1922 and the communists were in control. By the 1930s it was recovering its strength.

Japan

Japan had sided with the victors in the war and had done well. She gained Germany's Far Eastern colonies and experienced a trade boom. Also, because Europe was busy fighting it gave Japan a free hand in Asia. But Japan desperately needed more raw materials. She wanted to take these from her neighbours. Japan already controlled Korea.

Italy

Italy had changed sides at the beginning of the war as she was promised gains at the end of the war. In the 1930s she wanted to extend her empire in Africa.

China

Today China is a superpower but in the 1920s and 30s she was divided by civil war. She was weak and backward.

Questions

1 Which parts of the British Empire did Britain fear might be threatened and by which countries?

2 How do you think other countries would feel about a large and powerful communist country such as Russia?

3 Where would Japan invade to find the raw materials and markets she needed?

4 Can you work out from the map which country in Africa Italy decided to invade and add to her Empire?

5 Which country was looking to expand and saw China as a source of raw materials and markets?

Source A World Empires

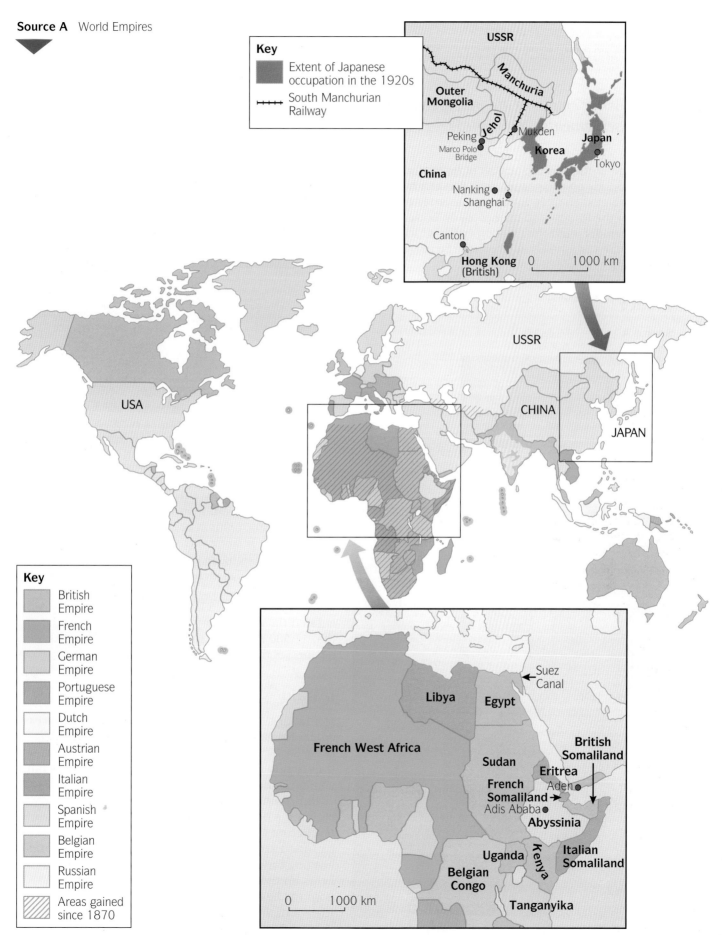

Key
- Extent of Japanese occupation in the 1920s
- South Manchurian Railway

USSR
Outer Mongolia
Manchuria
Jehol
Peking
Marco Polo Bridge
Mukden
Korea
Japan
Tokyo
China
Nanking
Shanghai
Canton
Hong Kong (British)

0   1000 km

USSR
CHINA
USA
JAPAN

Key
- British Empire
- French Empire
- German Empire
- Portuguese Empire
- Dutch Empire
- Austrian Empire
- Italian Empire
- Spanish Empire
- Belgian Empire
- Russian Empire
- Areas gained since 1870

Libya
Egypt
Suez Canal
French West Africa
Sudan
Eritrea
British Somaliland
French Somaliland
Aden
Adis Ababa
Abyssinia
Italian Somaliland
Uganda
Kenya
Belgian Congo
Tanganyika

0   1000 km

Memories of war

▶ *What emotions did people in different countries have as the peace settlements approached?*

At the end of the war the leaders of the victors had to meet to decide on the peace terms. You can read about this in the next chapter. Everyone was affected by the war, both the leaders and the people on both sides. To help you understand the emotions with which people from different countries approached the peace talks, study each example below.

France

Source A

1,358,000 soldiers killed
2,500,000 soldiers wounded
23,000 factories destroyed
5,600 km of railway line wrecked
300,000 houses destroyed

Source B   The main street of Pozieres before the war

Source C   The same scene after the battle of Pozieres, 1916

Source D   A propaganda poster of the sinking of the *Lusitania*

USA

Most Americans had wanted to stay out of the war. But the American Government found this more and more difficult. Public opinion began to change when the British liner *Lusitania* was sunk by a German U-boat and among the passengers drowned were 128 Americans. US merchant ships were also sunk. Finally British agents came up with evidence that Germany was encouraging Mexican rebels to invade Texas. The USA entered the war in April 1917. It has been calculated that 11,500 American servicemen were killed. At home, businesses made huge profits due to the war.

Britain

18 March 1915: A German submarine U-33 surfaces and orders the British steamship *The Brussels* to halt. *The Brussels* slows down, then suddenly it speeds up and tries to ram the submarine. The submarine dives but is damaged and turns away.

In Britain the Captain of *The Brussels*, Charles Fryatt, becomes a hero. The Germans decide to get their revenge on Captain Fryatt.

22 June 1916: 11p.m. *The Brussels* sails from Holland heading towards Britain. To hide from submarines the lights on the ship are put out. A bright light flashes from the beach and is followed by a rocket flare. At 12.46 a.m. five German destroyers surround and capture *The Brussels*.

26 July 1916: The Germans put Captain Fryatt on trial for being a 'franctireur' (guerrilla fighter – a charge similar to piracy). He is found guilty and executed the same day.

Source E The London Morning Post

Every captain of a ship has the right to defend his vessel. This death sentence is, in fact, murder.

The war cost Britain 750,000 soldiers killed, many more wounded and £8,700,000,000.

Germany

The German view of Captain Fryatt was very different. The British Navy was blockading Germany and causing much hardship and hunger. Germany was slowly being strangled. The Germans tried to do the same to Britain but the only way to do this was for her submarine fleet to sink Allied merchant ships. Submarines were meant to surface and give the passengers and crew a chance to abandon ship. The U-33 had done this but had been attacked by *The Brussels* without warning. So Captain Fryatt had broken international law and must be punished. The Germans said there were 58 such attacks on submarines in the first two years of the war. The cost of the war in German lives was nearly two million with more than four million wounded.

Source F Count Max Mongelas, a German politician during the war

Germany's preparations for war were on a considerably smaller scale than those made by France… An impression was produced in London that we were the aggressors

Austria-Hungary

The cost in lives was 1,200,000 killed and 3,600,000 wounded.

Examples like Source **G** caused very stong emotions and there were plenty of other stories of atrocities on both sides. The high number of dead and wounded people meant very few families did not suffer the pain of losing a loved one. Consequently, politicians were under great pressure from public opinion when it came to sorting out the peace terms.

Source G Vienna 1919, starving children wrapped in newspapers are taken to hospital

Questions

1 What kind of emotions did people in each of these countries have as the Peace Settlement approached?

2 What might be the first thing demanded in the Peace Settlement by a French person living in Pozieres? (Sources **B** and **C**.)

3 Does Source **D** appear to be propaganda?

4 Why are the German and British views of Captain Fryatt so different?

5 How long do you think the emotions aroused by the pain and suffering of war would last, into the 1920s, the 1930s, the 1940s or longer?

6 How would such emotions affect international relations?

2 The Peace Treaties

The Treaty of Versailles – The Peacemakers

 What were the aims of the peacemakers?

In January 1919 the leaders of the victorious countries met in Paris to decide on the terms of the peace treaties. The leaders of Britain, France and the USA were by far the most important and were known as the 'Big Three'. They were:

David Lloyd George – British Prime Minister
George Clemenceau – French Prime Minister
Woodrow Wilson – US President.

The Treaty of Versailles

The main treaty was to be the Treaty of Versailles which dealt with the future of Germany. The important questions which the 'Big Three' had to answer were:

1 Who was guilty of starting the war?
2 Should they put Kaiser Wilhelm (the ruler of Germany) on trial for starting the war?
3 Should Germany be forced to pay reparations? If so, how much?
4 Should Germany be allowed to keep any armed forces at all? If so, how many?
5 Should Germany be allowed to have any colonies? If not, should they become independent? Or should they come under the control of a new international organisation – the League of Nations?
6 What about the German-speaking people in Austria? Some Austrians might want to unite with Germany – should this be allowed?
7 What should happen to territory on the borders of Germany which both the Germans and neighbouring countries claimed (see Source **B**)?

To help understand the decisions of the 'Big Three' you need to know their aims and motives. First study the biography and viewpoint of Lloyd George and then decide from his point of view on an answer to each of the questions 1–7 above. Remember also the cost of the war for Britain and the memories and emotions you read about on pages 14–15. Then do the same from the viewpoints of Clemenceau and Wilson. Therefore, you need to make three sets of decisions. Your teacher may give you a chart to help you organise your decisions.

Source A The 'Big Three', Clemenceau, Wilson and Lloyd George after signing the Treaty, 28 June 1919

View 1 Lloyd George – Britain

Biography: David Lloyd George 1863–1945. He trained as a lawyer and became a Liberal MP in 1890. He became Prime Minister in 1916 and was an energetic war leader. He was a very clever speaker and politician and was known as 'the Welsh Wizard'.
Viewpoint: Lloyd George believed the war had been fought for the preservation of the British Empire. He was not in favour of harshly punishing Germany, but as a politician he had to think about the following:
1 The British public and press wanted Germany to be harshly punished.
2 He had just won the General Election by promising to 'make Germany pay!'
3 He feared that if Germany was crippled:
  • the French would dominate Europe;
  • Germany would not help stop the spread of communism;
  • Britain would lose Germany as its best customer.

Lloyd George wanted the USA to guarantee the new peace in Europe.

View 2 Clemenceau – France

Biography: George Clemenceau 1841–1929. Clemenceau was known as 'The Tiger' for his fierce attacks criticising the mistakes of the French Government. He became Prime Minister of France for a year, 1906–7. In 1917 the war was going badly and he

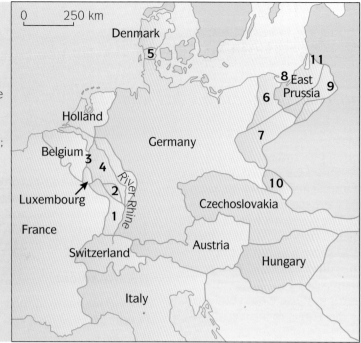

1 Alsace–Lorraine
Important industrial area; claimed by France (had been French until 1870).

2 Saar
Large coalfields; claimed by France but with a German population.

3 Eupen/Malmedy
Important coal and iron resources; claimed by Belgium (Belgium was neutral in 1914 and suffered badly when Germany invaded).

4 Rhineland
Claimed by France for protection, but had a German population.

5 Schleswig
Population a mixture of Germans (more in the South) and Danes (more in the North). Claimed by Denmark but German since the 1860s.

6 West Prussia
7 Posen and Thorn
German-speaking areas, claimed by Poland. Essential to give Poland access to the sea, but this would separate East Prussia from the rest of Germany.

8 Danzig
An important port; claimed by Poland but with a German-speaking population.

9 Allenstein/Marienwerder
10 Upper Silesia
Mixed population of Germans and Poles.

11 Memel
Between Lithuania and East Prussia, claimed by Lithuania.

was once again asked to become Prime Minister. He was a vigorous war leader who would not consider defeat.

Viewpoint: Clemenceau believed the war had been fought for the security of France and so Germany must now be weakened. France had suffered greatly in the war. Clemenceau's aims were:
1 to make sure Germany paid in full for the damage;
2 to regain Alsace–Lorraine which France had lost in the war of 1870–71;
3 to make sure Germany could not invade France;
4 Germany should lose territory;
5 to make the Rhineland independent.

View 3 Wilson – USA

Biography: Woodrow Wilson 1856–1924. He was a very religious man with a strong sense of right and wrong. When re-elected President in 1916 he promised to keep the USA out of the war.

By 1917 he had changed his mind.

Viewpoint: Wilson believed the war had been fought for democracy and national self-determination (the right of a people to govern their own country). Wilson had a vision, he called this vision the Fourteen Points. He believed the peace treaties should be based on these points. The old empires should go. The peace treaties must also be fair and not humiliate Germany.

President Wilson's Fourteen Points:

Aim: to prevent another war
1 No more secret treaties between countries.
2 The seas to be free to ships of all nations.
3 No restrictions on trade between countries.
4 All countries to reduce armaments.

Aim: to achieve self-determination (the right of each person to live in their own country)
5 Greater independence for colonies.
6 Russia to choose its own system of government.
7 Belgium to be independent again.
8 Alsace–Lorraine to be returned to France.
9 Italy's frontiers to be redrawn along lines of nationality.
10 Different nationalities in the Austro-Hungarian Empire to be allowed self-government.
11 People in the Balkans to be free to form their own countries.
12 Independence for non-Turkish people in the Turkish Empire.
13 Poland to be independent.
14 An international organisation to be set up to settle disputes.

When you have completed the task and have three sets of decisions, work out how often your three leaders agreed on the questions. If your answer is very rarely or not at all then you have discovered the problem of the Treaty of Versailles – the 'Big Three' did not agree. Read again the first line of the viewpoint of each leader to see the difference.

Questions

1 Look at the following of Wilson's Fourteen Points, numbers **1**, **4**, **5**, **6**, **10**, **11** and **14**. For each point say how different it was from the way the world was run before the war.

2 If other countries were to gain land in which some of the population were German, how could a German leader use this to take the land back?

The Treaty of Versailles – The terms

 Did the Peacemakers get the terms they wanted?

After four months of often bitter negotiations between the Allies the terms were agreed. President Wilson was exhausted and ill and refused to listen to concerns that the terms were too harsh. On 7 May the terms were announced. The Germans were horrified. At first Germany refused to sign but Allied soldiers were ready to invade and there was hunger in Germany because of the Allied blockade. As a result, on 28 June 1919 Germany signed the Treaty of Versailles. Study the terms and use what you learnt about the views of the 'Big Three' to answer the questions on the terms.

The terms of the Treaty

The War Guilt Clause

Clause 231 '… Germany accepts the responsibility for causing all the loss and damage to which the allied governments and their nationals have been subjected as a consequence of the war imposed upon them by the aggression of Germany and her allies.'

Reparations

Germany was to pay compensation for the damage caused by war, for example the cost of rebuilding homes and factories and even for pensions and disability payments to British sailors and soldiers. The amount was later fixed at £6,600,000,000.

Disarmament

The German armed forces were to be cut to an army of only 100,000 men and a small navy, with no tanks, war planes or submarines.

New borders

Germany lost territory (Source **A**). The new state of Poland was given part of West Prussia, Posen and Silesia so that a 'Polish corridor' gave Poland access to the sea. This meant that German East Prussia was cut off from the rest of Germany. The German speaking

Source A The new borders of Germany

Key
- Germany 1914
- Land taken from Germany
- Land under League of Nations control
- Demilitarised zone

Denmark

Lithuania

North Schleswig

Danzig

East Prussia (Part of Germany)

West Prussia

Germany

Posen

Poland

Belgium

Upper Silesia

Rhineland

Saarland

Lorraine

France

Alsace

0   400 km

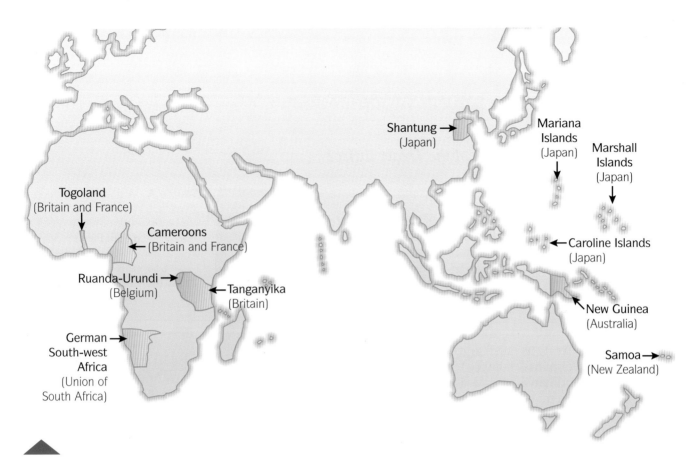

Source B The German colonies which became League of Nations Mandates

city of Danzig was made a free city under the control of the League of Nations. Alsace and Lorraine were returned to France. The Saarland, which was rich in coal, was to be controlled by the League of Nations for 15 years. The Rhineland stayed part of Germany but it was occupied by Allied troops for 15 years and no German soldiers were allowed there. In some areas of mixed population votes (plebiscites) were held. For example in Schleswig the northern part voted to be part of Denmark and the south voted to stay part of Germany. Also Germany was forbidden to unite with Austria.

The German Overseas Empire

Germany lost her colonies (Source B). They were to be called 'mandates' and shared out among the victors who would run them on behalf of the League of Nations.

The League of Nations

This was a new organisation, its main task was to sort out problems between nations and so prevent wars.

National groups from all over the world came to see President Wilson in Paris and ask for his support for the right to govern themselves. Some groups in Europe were successful. But Britain and France did not like the idea and so the peoples in the British and French Empires did not achieve national self-determination.

Questions

1 Which of the 'Big Three'– Lloyd George, Clemenceau or Wilson – most supported the idea of Germany's guilt and which was least keen on the idea?

2 Each of the 'Big Three' argued for reparations to be set at different amounts, who do you think argued for the highest amount and who argued for the lowest?

3 Which of the 'Big Three' most wanted strict controls of Germany's armed forces?

4 Which of these changes went against Wilson's idea of national self-determination?

5 Which of the 'Big Three' wanted German colonies to be prepared for independence?

6 Which of the three leaders had a vision to remake the world in which the League of Nations was to play a key role?

7 How far did each of the three leaders get what they wanted at the Peace Conference? To answer this compare their aims on pages 16–17 with the terms on these pages. For President Wilson you can try to work out which of his Fourteen Points were achieved.

► *How did people's view of the Treaty differ?*

At the time people had very different views on the Treaty. Some people thought the Treaty let Germany off too easily, others thought it was too harsh and would only lead to another war.

German view

Germans saw the Treaty as harsh and vindictive. Most Germans felt angry and humiliated. Germany had agreed to a ceasefire in November 1918 so that a peace treaty based on Wilson's Fourteen Points could be negotiated. By June 1919 they believed they were being forced to sign a treaty not based on the Fourteen Points. They called this a 'diktat' – a dictated peace, which was harsh and unfair. Some Germans believed their army had not been defeated but tricked into surrendering by socialist politicians and Jews. Germany felt that it had been 'stabbed in the back'. The three issues which most angered the Germans were:

1 The 'War Guilt Clause' which put all the blame for causing the war on Germany.
2 Reparations, in 1921 Germany was ordered to pay £6,600,000,000. This was a massive sum and many people believed Germany had no way of paying it.
3 The loss of 13 % of German territory containing 7.3 million people and all of her overseas colonies. Germany was now cut in two, divided by the land given to Poland. Germany also lost 75 % of her iron ore and zinc deposits, 28 % of her coal and 17 % of her grain and potato production.

Sources **A–D** show the German view.

Source D From a statement by Ebert, Germany's President, May 1919

> The German people… trusted the promise given by the Allies that the peace would be a peace of right on the basis of President Wilson's Fourteen Points. What is now given us in the peace terms is a contradiction of the promise given… Such a dictated peace will provoke fresh hatred between the nations and, in the course of history, fresh killing.

Source A A dwarfish Clemenceau gleefully tears up a document which reads 'Armistice on the basis of Wilson's Fourteen Points'

Source B Michel (Germany) signing the 'Peace of Justice of the Entente'. The ink bottle bears the word 'Blood is a very special liquid'

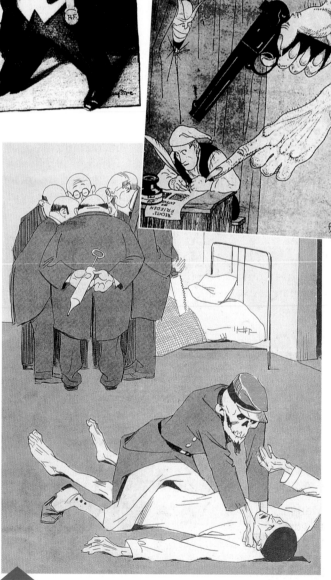

Source C While the doctors confer about Germany's future, France tries to see she doesn't have one

Other views

The views of those on the winning side varied. Most people thought Germany had got what it deserved (Sources **E** and **G**).

Source E On 16 June 1919 Clemenceau replied to German attempts to alter the terms before signing them

The war was the greatest crime against humanity that any nation has ever committed… not less than seven million dead lie buried in Europe, while more than twenty million others carry upon them the evidence of wounds and sufferings… Justice is what the German delegation asks for and says that Germany has been promised. Justice is what Germany shall have. But it must be justice for all. There must be justice for the dead and wounded and for those who have been orphaned and bereaved. There must be justice for those millions whose homes and land, ships and property German savagery has destroyed… Somebody must suffer for the consequences of the war. Is it to be Germany, or only the peoples she has wronged?

A different view was held by the British economist John Maynard Keynes. In 1920 he wrote an important book called *The Economic Consequences of the Peace*. This warned that the treaties would prevent the European economy recovering from the damage the war had done. (Source **F**.)

Source F *The Economic Consequences of the Peace* by John Maynard Keynes

The Treaties include nothing to make the defeated Central Empires (Germany and Austria) into good neighbours, nothing to stabilise the new States of Europe, nothing to reclaim Russia… no arrangements for restoring the disordered finances of France and Italy… The danger facing us, therefore, is the drop of the standard of life of the European population to a point which will mean actual starvation for some.

Many modern historians emphasise the problems faced by the peacemakers and are less critical of the Treaty. For example even before the peace negotiations began the Austro-Hungarian Empire had collapsed and nationalists had set up new governments in Czechoslovakia, Poland and Yugoslavia.

Source G British cartoon from Punch magazine in 1919 shows the problems of Germany being dealt with by the Treaty of Versailles

Questions

1 How do Sources **A** and **B** agree with Source **D**?

2 Which of the Allied leaders did the Germans most blame for what they saw as harsh peace terms? Support your answer by referring to Sources **A** and **E**.

3 In Source **D** what two reasons does Ebert give as to why the Treaty of Versailles was not justified?

4 Ebert (Source **D**) and Clemenceau (Source **E**) talk about a different sort of justice. First explain how their views of justice differ, then explain why they differ.

5 How might a German politician answer Clemenceau's last two sentences in Source **E**?

6 Many modern historians are sympathetic to the peacemakers. Why do views about past events such as the Treaty of Versailles change over the years?

7 In Source **G** what is the angel of peace doing? Is the cartoonist justifying the peace terms?

Justifying the Treaty of Versailles

▶ *Was the Treaty of Versailles justified at the time?*

'Justified at the time' means did the Allies have good reasons for the terms they imposed. To decide this involves asking two questions:

1 Were the aims of the Allies reasonable?
2 If so, were the terms a fair way of achieving their aims?

Ever since the Treaty was signed people have argued whether it was justified (reasonable) at the time. These opposing views are shown below:

Source A   Lloyd George signs the Treaty watched by other leaders

No, it was not justified

1 The Allies tricked Germany into signing an armistice by letting them believe the peace treaty would be based on Wilson's Fourteen Points which did not refer to guilt or reparations.

2 The German people were made to pay for the sins of the former rulers, the Kaiser and his government, but they were now gone.

3 It was an act of revenge which can only lead to another act of revenge in reply.

4 The Allies took part in the arms race, the Alliance system and empire building – these all helped cause the war, therefore Germany should not take all the blame.

5 The amount of reparation was unrealistic, it was far too much and would cripple the German economy and ordinary men, women and children would go hungry.

6 The tiny army Germany was allowed by the Treaty meant she would be at the mercy of her neighbours.

7 The loss of territory meant a large part of Germany's wealth was taken from her and 7.3 million Germans now lived in a foreign country, this was not self-determination.

Yes, it was justified

1 The Germans were not interested in Wilson's Fourteen Points when he first talked about them. Indeed the Germans forced a very harsh treaty on Russia in 1918 which took no notice of Wilson's Fourteen Points.

2 The German people had supported the Kaiser, they cannot hide behind the acts of their former rulers.

3 If you do wrong you should be punished – it is as simple as that – otherwise you will do it again.

4 It was Germany which encouraged Austria-Hungary to go to war with Serbia, this started the ball rolling.

5 Germany had caused the damage so she should pay for it. For example, many French coalmines had been put out of action, so while they were being repaired France was to receive coal from German mines in the Saarland. In any case in the 1930s Hitler found such large sums of money to rearm Germany.

6 The German army had been too powerful and made Germany an aggressive military state, so it was a bad influence which had to be removed to make Germany peaceful.

7 Some of the areas of Germany were of mixed races, some areas voted to leave Germany, some areas had once belonged to other countries, some land was needed by Poland to give it access to the sea.

Source B The Treaty of Versailles means no more sunshine for Germany

Now decide if you think the Treaty of Versailles was justified at the time. The views on page 22 may help you. Using a copy of the chart below, first decide if each aim was reasonable and, if it was, then decide if the term that resulted was a fair way of achieving that aim (or was it unfair as it was too harsh or would lead to problems later on?) If you decide an aim is not reasonable, then the term cannot be fair.

Do your answers show that you think the Treaty of Versailles was:

  a justified at the time?
  b partly justified, but other parts not?
  c not justified?

Whether or not the Treaty was justified, at the time the Germans believed it was not. Consequently, the aim of all German leaders after 1919 was to reverse the Treaty. How the Allies reacted to this changed with time and depended on who the leader of Germany was.

Aims	Was the aim reasonable? Yes/No	Terms	Was the term a fair way of achieving the aim? Yes/No
1 a) Germany to be made solely responsible for the war.		'War Guilt' Clause.	
b) Germany should pay for the damage.		Reparations (later fixed at £6,600,000,000).	
2 Germany must never be able to start a war.		German army only 100,000, small navy, no tanks, war planes or submarines.	
3 People should have the right to national self-determination.		Rhineland to be demilitarised. Germany to lose areas containing Poles, Czechs, French, Belgians and others. In total Germany lost 13% of its land and 7.3 million people. In some areas votes were held, e.g. in Upper Silesia the western half stayed with Germany, the eastern half went to Poland.	

*Q*uestions

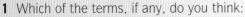

1 Which of the terms, if any, do you think:
  a) was most unjustified?
  b) was most necessary?
  c) would cause most problems in the future?

2 What point is the cartoonist making in Source **B**?

The other Peace Treaties

▶ How were the other defeated countries treated?

What does the cartoonist in Source **A** suggest will happen to the other defeated countries? See if you agree with his predictions when you have studied these pages.

Treaties were made with each of the other defeated nations – Austria-Hungary, Bulgaria and Turkey. All of these countries lost land, were forced to reduce their armies and were ordered to pay reparations. New countries were created – Czechoslovakia, Poland and Yugoslavia. The 'Big Three' were not so involved in these peace treaties, most of the work was done by officials and foreign ministers.

Source A A British cartoon taken from the Daily Express comments on the fate of the defeated countries at the Peace Conference

Source B The new countries of Europe

Treaty of St Germain with Austria 1919

1 Large areas of land were lost to the three new states of Czechoslovakia, Poland and Yugoslavia as well as smaller areas to Italy.
2 Army limited to 30,000 men.
3 Reparations to be paid.

Treaty of Neuilly with Bulgaria 1919

1 Land lost to Yugoslavia and Greece.
2 Army limited to 20,000 men.
3 Reparations to be paid.

Treaty of Trianon with Hungary 1920

1 Land lost to Romania, Czechoslovakia and Yugoslavia.
2 Army limited to 20,000 men.
3 Reparations to be paid.

Source C Mustapha Kemal (centre). When he came to power, Kemal took the name 'Ataturk' – Father of the Turks.

Source D From a Speech by Mustapha Kemal

The Sultan and his government are prisoners in the hands of the Allies. We are about to lose our country. I have come to seek your help and save the situation… We are fighting with our backs to the wall, but we will fight to the end. We demand the right of every sovereign (independent) state to be free within our own boundaries. We ask nothing more and nothing less.

Treaty of Sevres with Turkey 1920 (replaced in 1923 by the Treaty of Lausanne)

1 Turkey lost Eastern Thrace and Smyrna to Greece. She also lost her Empire – land in Palestine, Jordan, Syria and Iraq.
2 Lost control of the Straits into the Black Sea.
3 Reparations to be paid.

Turkey and the Peace Treaties

All of these treaties created problems and many people wanted to change them. The only one which was changed immediately was the treaty with Turkey. In 1919 the ruler of Turkey was the Sultan, but there were British, French and Italian troops stationed in Turkey and the Sultan did what the Allies told him. In 1920 he agreed to the Treaty of Sevres. Many Turks were angered by this and refused to accept the Sultan's rule. In 1920 a young army officer, Mustapha Kemal, set up a rival government and prepared to free Turkey (Sources **C** and **D**).

In Britain *The Times* newspaper described Kemal and his nationalist supporters as 'a minority of adventurers, criminals and fanatics'. But *The Times* was wrong. In 1921–22 Kemal defeated the Greek armies in Turkey. The occupying French and Italian troops withdrew, leaving only 4,000 British troops in Chanak facing 36,000 Turkish troops.

The British agreed to discuss a new peace treaty which was signed at Lausanne in Switzerland in 1923. Reparations were cancelled and Eastern Thrace, Smyrna and control of the Straits were returned to Turkey. Over one million Greeks living in Turkey were forced to leave their homes, and about 400,000 Turks left Greece. This massive movement of people did to some extent sort out the problem of Turks and Greeks living in the same areas. But the problem was not sorted out in the rest of Europe.

Questions

1 a) Do you think the cartoonist who drew Source **A** was correct? Did the other countries receive similar treatment to Germany?
  b) Which important clause in the Treaty of Versailles which angered the Germans, was absent from these treaties.

2 Why do you think Britain and France took control of the Turks' Arab empire instead of giving independence to the Arabs who had helped the Allies in the war?

3 a) What impression does Source **C** give of Mustapha Kemal?
  b) In Source **D** how does Kemal justify his fight to overthrow the Sultan?

Consequences and future problems

▶ *How had Europe changed? What problems beset Europe in 1920?*

By the end of 1919 the new shape of Europe was emerging. Before the First World War there had been five great powers in Europe, like five boxers in one ring. But Austria-Hungary had collapsed; Russia was out of the ring for the time being, occupied with civil war at home; Germany had been knocked down, and its hands were tied by the terms of the Treaty of Versailles. On the fringes of Europe, the Turkish Empire had also collapsed. Of the former great powers, only Britain and France were left – both exhausted – but still on their feet.

There were also the new, independent countries, such as Poland, Czechoslovakia, Yugoslavia and the Baltic States of Lithuania, Estonia and Finland. Some of these countries were weak and poor; it was clear

they would be no match for Germany or Russia should either of them recover their strength. One of the aims of the peacemakers had been to allow national self-determination, the right of national groups to form their own country. But this rarely worked in practice. It was usually impossible to draw clear borders between different national groups as they often lived in the same region, or town or even village. The following case study shows the problem.

Case study – Central and South Eastern Europe

To understand the problems in this area of Europe study the sources and answer the questions which follow.

Source A
The patchwork of races and nationalities in 1918

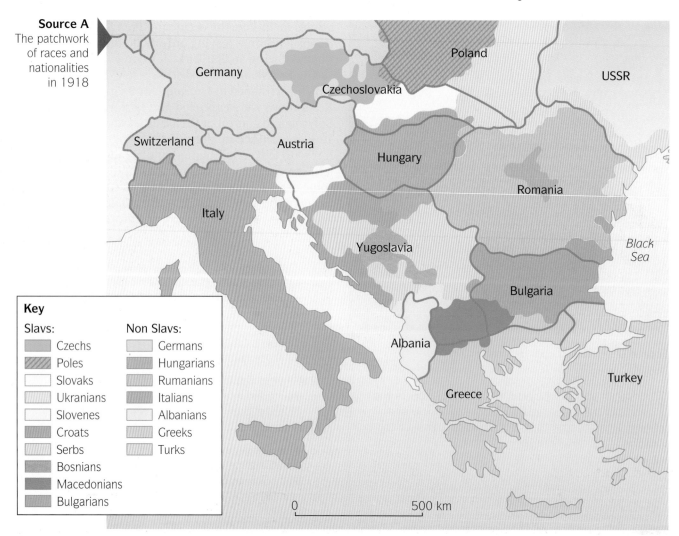

Key

Slavs:
- Czechs
- Poles
- Slovaks
- Ukranians
- Slovenes
- Croats
- Serbs
- Bosnians
- Macedonians
- Bulgarians

Non Slavs:
- Germans
- Hungarians
- Rumanians
- Italians
- Albanians
- Greeks
- Turks

0   500 km

Source B   In 1914 about half the people on the continent were minorities living in a country ruled by a different national group. After the Peace Treaties only one quarter were minorities. But the problem still existed.

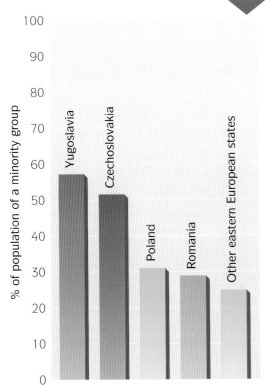

Source C   National Groups in Czechoslovakia in the 1920s.

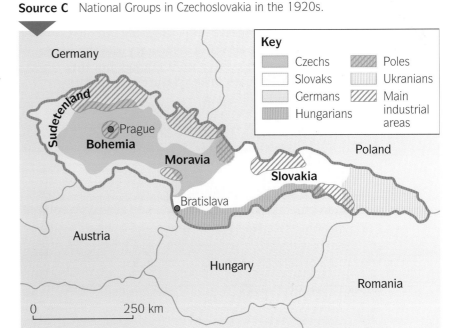

Source D   1921: Hungarians march to protest against the loss of the land given to neighbouring countries under the Treaty of Trianon

uestions

1 Answer the following using Source **A**.
  a) Find examples where it would not be practical to make a country out of every area inhabited by a national group.
  b) Without moving people how many countries would need to be formed to make sure there was not more than one national group in a country?
  c) Find examples of a national group which did not have its own state but was spread amongst three states and another group spread amongst four states.
  d) Why could the borders of Hungary not contain all Hungarians?
  e) Which country contained most national groups?

  f) If Germany wanted to expand to include all Germans within her borders, which countries had most to fear?
  g) Which national group lived in the areas where most of Czechoslovakia's heavy industry was sited (see Source **C**)?

2 In 1920–21 Romania, Czechoslovakia and Yugoslavia signed the 'Little Entente'. Which country were they trying to protect themselves against.

3 In Czechoslovakia which national group do you think posed the biggest threat to the Czechs? Explain why.

4 Did the Peace Treaties help reduce the problem of minority national groups?

The problem in Czechoslovakia

Perhaps the key state in central Europe was Czechoslovakia. Unlike the other new states it was a democracy and the Allies hoped it would help stabilise this part of Europe. But the Slovaks and Sudeten Germans believed the Czech majority did not treat them fairly (Source **E**).

Source E 1919 Lloyd George comments on the plans for the new state of Czechoslovakia

The Allied powers are creating a state inhabited by not only 6.5 million Czechs, but also some 3.5 million Germans, who will revolt from the very outset... also 2 million Slovaks who, in spite of their affinity (close relationship) with the Czech nation, have their own language and have nothing in common with Bohemia and Moravia (Czech areas).

This problem of minorities also existed in northern Europe where Germans, Lithuanians and Ukranians now lived in Poland. Between 1918 and 1921 Poland grew in size by fighting her neighbours and seizing territory. These problem areas made Europe unstable. Some of these problems still exist today, in the 1990s Serbs and Croats have fought bitterly in the former Yugoslavia.

Think about the people listed below, living in Europe in 1920. They all lived in a problem area (see Source **F**) or had reason to hate the Peace Treaties. Discuss what hopes or fears each might have had about the future and decide which problem area was most likely to be a cause of the next war.

Source F

1 German factory worker living in the port of Danzig. This had been part of Germany but in 1919 it was made a 'Free City' under the control of the League of Nations.

2 German teacher in the Sudetenland. This was a German-speaking area, part of the old Austro-Hungarian Empire. In 1919 it became part of Czechoslovakia.

5 Corporal in the German army who had been born in Austria and fought for Germany in the war. He dreamed of the day when Germany would become great again and recover the land it had lost.

3 Hungarian soldier who had fought against Romania in the war. He lived in Transylvania, in eastern Hungary, which became part of Romania in 1919.

6 Italian shop owner living in the city of Fiume in Yugoslavia. Italy had been promised Fiume in return for joining the Allies in the war, but this promise was broken.

7 A Russian peasant living in Bessarabia which was invaded in 1919 and became part of Poland.

4 Polish coalminer living in the city of Teschen and working in nearby coalmines. Both Czechoslovakia and Poland had good reason to claim the area. The Allies bullied both countries into accepting an agreement whereby Poland kept Teschen and Czechoslovakia got the coalmines and the railway station.

At the time it was probably impossible to solve these problems (Source **G**).

Source G A comment by President Wilson's advisor, Colonel E House

Empires cannot be shattered and new states raised upon their ruins without disturbance. To create new boundaries is always to create new troubles... While I should have preferred a different peace, I doubt whether it could have been made... We have had to deal with a situation full of difficulties and one which could be met only by an unselfish and idealistic spirit, which was almost wholly absent and which was too much to expect of men come together at such a time and for such a purpose.

Other problems

There were also other problems in Europe. Much of Europe was in chaos. Millions of people were unemployed; returning soldiers could not find work, and others lost their jobs when factories stopped making weapons. Industry and trade were in decline. In some countries, money lost its value, so buying and selling was difficult. Most goods were moved by rail, but much of the European railway system was in ruins. Production of vital supplies such as grain and coal was low, and people were already starving in Germany and Austria. Then, in 1919, an influenza virus hit Europe. Hungry people have little resistance to germs and the 'Spanish flu' spread rapidly. Twenty-seven million people died in the epidemic.

Source H A German cartoon showing Clemenceau leading the German delegation Versailles towards two hotel buses. The Germans ask 'Where is he taking us?' One bus is labelled 'Peace Hotel', the other is the 'Next War' hotel.

Questions

1 What fact do Sources **C** (on page 27) and **E** disagree on? How do you account for this difference?

2 **a)** According to Colonel House (Source **G**) why was a different peace settlement not reached in 1919?

   b) Was Colonel House correct in saying the peacemakers faced a situation 'full of difficulties'? Name some of the difficulties.

   c) Would the people in Source **F** be likely to have the 'unselfish and idealistic spirit' that Colonel House claimed was necessary?

3 Do you think the Peace Treaties decided which bus Europe would take? (Source **H**.)

4 Write a brief newspaper report titled 'Europe 1920 – Problems'. Base your report on the following paragraph openings, and place them in what you think is their order of importance:

There is hunger and starvation...
The new countries of Europe...
There are problems in Czechoslovakia...
Unemployment is...
Spanish influenza...
Many countries contain national minorities...
Another war could be caused by...

5 Use Sources **A** (on page 26) and **E** to make up more people living in problem areas like those in Source **F**.

3 The post-war world

War debts and reparations

▶ *How did war debts and reparations affect international relations?*

War debts

One thing which caused continual problems between countries after the war was money. War debts were owed but countries struggled to make the repayments. France, Russia, Italy and Belgium had borrowed from Britain and the USA, Britain had also borrowed heavily from the USA. The amounts of money owed were huge (Source **A**).

Source A The war debts owed

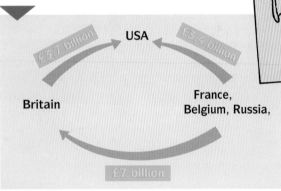

The Allies did not agree about the problem of war debts:

American view

Loans were given in good faith and so should be repaid.

British view

Loans were all part of the war effort and should be cancelled, but if the USA insisted on being paid then Britain would collect her war debts from France and others.

French view

They would pay as long as Germany paid the reparations awarded to France by the Treaty of Versailles.

So the problem of war debts was closely linked with the problem of reparations (Source **B**).

Source B 'Debts of War' showing Germany supporting France, France supporting Britain and Britain supporting the USA

Reparations

The amount Germany had to pay in reparations was fixed in 1921 at £6,600,000,000, to be paid in annual instalments. Germany paid the first instalment of £50 million, but in 1922 nothing was paid.

The Germans claimed they did not have the money, but the French Prime Minister, Poincare, believed this was just an excuse. In January 1923 he sent French soldiers to occupy the Ruhr area of Germany (Source **C**).

Source **C** French troops enter the Ruhr

Belgium also sent troops. The Ruhr was the industrial heart of Germany, producing three quarters of the country's coal and steel. Poincare was determined to take what Germany owed to France (Source **D**).

We are going to look for coal, that's all!… We have no intention of strangling Germany or ruining her, we only want to obtain from her what we can reasonably expect her to provide.

It was not that easy. The Germans were bitterly resentful. German workers in the Ruhr went on strike and adopted a policy of passive resistance. This meant that they would not co-operate with the French (Source **E**).

Source **E**   From Weimar Eyewitness by Egon Larsen

Wherever foreign soldiers appeared, German workers downed tools. The trains stopped running, the steelworks and factories emptied, the miners went home, farmers hid their food stocks, many shopkeepers locked up their premises… life came to a standstill.

The French brought in their own workers, but this did not solve the problem. They even tried to persuade the people in the Rhineland to set up a separate state, but the attempt failed.

The occupation of the Ruhr put a tremendous strain on the Germany economy. Before long, it cracked. The value of the mark (German currency) fell until it was almost worthless. At the end of 1923 the new German Chancellor, Gustav Stresemann realised that Germany had to co-operate with its former enemies, and he ended passive resistance in the Ruhr.

Britain and the USA strongly disapproved of the French invasion of the Ruhr and relations between the old Allies suffered.

Meanwhile an international committee met to examine Germany's economic problems. It was headed by an American, Charles Dawes. In 1924 it recommended that:
• reparations should be paid at a reduced rate;
• the German currency should be reorganised;
• an international loan should be raised to help Germany.

Source **F**   American money goes round in circles.

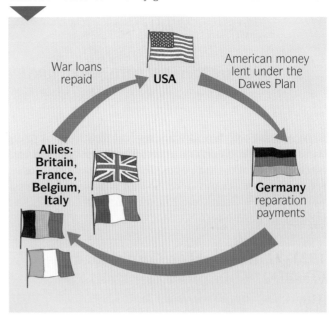

Stresemann accepted the Dawes Plan and American loans poured into Germany, enabling it to pay some of the reparations bill and restart industries. However, this was an artificial way of paying debts – the American money was simply going round in circles (Source **F**). When the Dawes Plan ended in 1929 a new plan, the Young Plan, was arranged to deal with reparations. It reduced reparations by three quarters and gave Germany until 1988 to pay them off.

Questions

1   Which of the countries in Source **A** owing money to the USA believed it should not repay any money at all? Why?

2   Which of the views on war debts, American, British or French, do you think was:
a) correct? **b)** most realistic?

3   Do the figures in Source **A** support the view of war debts shown in Source **B**?

4   According to the Treaty of Versailles France was acting legally when it occupied the Ruhr. Why then do you think America and Britain strongly disapproved of what France did?

5   In Source **F** what would happen if the American banks wanted back the money lent to Germany under the Dawes Plan?

Treaties and pacts in the 1920s

▶ **What treaties and pacts were signed in the 1920s?**

Between the two world wars several treaties and pacts were signed between countries. These are referred to often in the following pages. To avoid repeating the terms they are set out here. So you will need to refer to these pages from time to time – unless you can remember all the terms!

1921–22 Washington Conference (Treaty)

Aim: Naval disarmament.
Between November 1921 and February 1922 the USA organised a conference to discuss naval disarmament and tension in the Pacific and Far East. Two treaties were signed:

1 Washington Treaty (Five Power Treaty) – this limited the size of navies to:

	USA	Britain	Japan	France	Italy
Tonnes	525,000	525,000	300,000	175,000	175,000

2 The Nine Power Pact – this agreed not to invade China.

Rapallo Treaty April 1922

Aim: Co-operation between Germany and Russia.
Germany and Russia agreed:

1 to establish friendly relations;
2 to denounce reparations;
3 on economic co-operation;
4 on secret military co-operation.

Source A A modern historian Sally Marks comments:

On the Russian plains, far from prying eyes… Germany could and did build factories, produce the airplanes, poison gas, and tanks forbidden by the Versailles Treaty, test them, and train military personnel, both German and Russian, in their use. While this mutually beneficial arrangement had its ups and downs, it flourished throughout the twenties.

Locarno Pact 1925

Aim: To make Europe a safer place.
This was signed by many countries including Britain, France, Germany, Belgium and Italy. Many people believed 'the spirit of Locarno' promised an end to the feelings of revenge and bitterness and meant a period of peace (Source **B**). The most important terms were:

1 Germany, France and Belgium agreed that their borders were final (fixed). Britain and Italy guaranteed this.
2 The Rhineland was to remain demilitarised.
3 France promised to protect Poland and Czechoslovakia if attacked by Germany.
4 Germany was to join the League of Nations.

Source B Memories of a French journalist

I was drunk with joy. It seemed too good to be true that Germany, our enemy of yesterday, had actually signed the pact. From now on, no more fears for the future! No more war! I was not alone in my blind enthusiasm. Everyone in Locarno was jubilant.

Kellogg-Briand Pact 1928

Aim: To renounce the use of warfare.
This was signed by over forty nations who agreed not to use warfare to settle disputes (Source **C**).

Source C Article 1 of the Kellogg-Briand Pact

The High Contracting Parties declare… that they condemn recourse to war for the solution of international controversies (disputes) and renounce it as an instrument of national policy in their relations with one another.

This pact was a show of goodwill but there was no way of enforcing it. Indeed some nations appeared to have no intention of giving up warfare (Source **D**).

Source D 'Those Disquieting Sounds' an American cartoon, October 1929

Verdict

These treaties and pacts were only of any value so long as the countries which signed them kept their word. It was easy for countries to say they wanted peace and co-operation and would not go to war. But if they had aggressive aims then warfare was a useful means of achieving them. For example soon after signing the Kellogg-Briand Pact, some countries, notably Japan and Italy, used warfare to get what they wanted.

Source E The Treaties and pacts signed in the 1920s

Questions

1 Which country that signed the Washington Treaty (and was led at Versailles by one of the 'Big Three') would have been most unhappy about the size of fleet it was allowed?

2 a) In Source **A** what does 'mutually beneficial' mean?
   b) Why were Germany and Russia not worried about breaking the terms of the Treaty of Versailles (Source **A**)?

3 In Source **B** what does the phrase 'blind enthusiasm' tell you about the journalist's view of the Locarno Pact?

4 a) According to the wording in Article 1 (Source **C**) how far will the nations signing the Kellogg-Briand Pact go to make sure it is kept?
   b) In Source **D** does the turkey (world peace) seem worried? Why?
   c) Use the 'Verdict' to help you judge how accurate the prediction in Source **D** was.

5 Are Sources **A**, **B** and **D** optimistic or pessimistic about the pacts and treaties signed?

France searches for security

▶ **Why was France so afraid of Germany?**
What steps did France take to defend herself?

French fears

France knew that sooner or later Germany would recover from the war. Many French people were convinced that when Germany recovered she would attack France. The reasons why they feared such an attack are outlined below.

Reason 1

At Versailles Clemenceau had failed to really weaken Germany. When Germany recovered she would be stronger than France (Sources **A** and **B**).

Source A The strength of France and Germany in 1914 and 1938–9

	1914		1938–9	
	France	**Germany**	**France**	**Germany**
Troops	3,500,000	8,500 000	800,000	800,000
Reserve troops			4,600,000	2,200,000
Aircraft			600	4,500
Steel production (tons)	4,333,000	17,024,000	6,200,000	20,500,000
Coal production (tons)	40,800,000	279,000,000	46,500,000	169,200,000

Source B The Historian, AJP Taylor from his book *The Origins of the Second World War*, 1969

Germany remained by far the greatest Power on the continent of Europe… (it) was greatest in population – 65 million against 40 million in France, the only other major Power. German superiority was greater still in the economic resources of coal and steel which in modern times together made up power… nothing could prevent the Germans from overshadowing Europe, even if they did not plan to do so.

Reason 2

France believed the River Rhine was the best barrier against a German attack. So they wanted control of the Rhine and its bridges (Source **C**).

Source C Clemenceau explains how France is open to attack

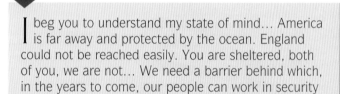

I beg you to understand my state of mind… America is far away and protected by the ocean. England could not be reached easily. You are sheltered, both of you, we are not… We need a barrier behind which, in the years to come, our people can work in security to rebuild the ruins. That barrier is the river Rhine

But France failed to get Britain and the USA to agree to this idea or to the idea of a separate Rhineland state. Instead, Germany had to accept that Allied troops were to occupy the area west of the Rhine for 15 years, and that a 50 mile strip east of the Rhine would be demilitarised (no German troops or fortresses would be allowed there).

Reason 3

France failed to get either the USA or Britain to guarantee help against a German attack. France did not believe it could rely on the League of Nations for protection. Russia was France's traditional ally, but Russia was now communist and did not want to ally with France.

Reason 4

Ever since their defeat in 1871 the French were obsessed with 'denatalite' (declining birthrate). France believed the birthrate was the key to her survival. But in France the birthrate was declining (Source **D**).

Source D Population (millions)

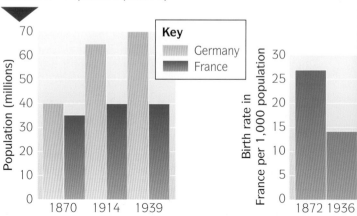

Reason 5

France had been invaded by Germany twice in living memory, in 1871 and 1914. The damage done in the First World War was vast (Source **E**).

Source E   The damage to France during the war

1,356,000	soldiers killed
23,000	factories destroyed
2,000,000	people forced to flee from their homes
90%	of coal and iron industry destroyed
£5,392,000,000	spent on defending France.

The search for security

France tried to find security in five ways:

1 During the 1920s France kept a large army, and formed alliances with Germany's other neighbours: Belgium (1920); Poland (1921); Czechoslovakia (1924); Romania (1926) and Yugoslavia (1927).
2 France was determined to recover the reparations owed by Germany. So when Germany failed to keep up the payments France invaded the Ruhr to take what France was owed but this action failed.
3 In 1925 France joined with other European powers at Locarno in Switzerland in an attempt to secure peace by signing the Locarno Treaties (see page 32).

4 A massive propaganda campaign tried to increase the birthrate in France. Films, postcards and books all warned of the dangers (Source **F**). Mothers with at least six children were awarded prizes and medals. People who sold contraceptives were imprisoned.
5 Between 1930–35 France built the Maginot Line, this was a massive line of fortresses along the border with Germany (Source **G**).

Source F   A French postcard 'A good bayonet-thrust!', many such postcards were produced and linked virility with military success

Source G   A cutaway part of the Maginot Line, only the gun casements were above ground

Questions

1 Look at Source **A**.
  a) What do the figures show about Germany's industrial strength compared with that of France?
  b) What do the figures for 1938–9 suggest about what France believed to be important for defence?
  c) Why are the steel and coal manufacturing figures important?

2 a) According to AJP Taylor (Source **B**) why did Germany remain a threat after the First World War?
  b) Why did Clemenceau think that control of the Rhine was so important (Source **C**)?

3 Does Source **D** help you decide if the campaign to increase the birthrate was successful?

4 Which of the five attempts to find security could France most rely on?

4 Countries and problems

Britain and the world 1919–33

 What problems did Britain face abroad?
What policy did Britain adopt towards the rest of the world?

Britain's strength?

In 1919 the future appeared bright for Britain. With her Empire she seemed immensely strong. She had done well from the Peace Treaties and now controlled large parts of the former German and Turkish Empires. The British Empire now covered nearly a quarter of the world's land surface (Source **A**). She had an army of 5.5 million men and the largest navy. Her rivals were either defeated or friendly. She was owed more money by her European allies than she herself owed America. Britain hoped that the League of Nations, led by Britain and the USA, would keep world peace. Britain could then concentrate on running her Empire. These were the hopes of the British Government. But the truth was that Britain faced a number of problems and the hopes of a bright future were quickly shattered.

Concerns and problems

Study the concerns and problems Britain faced. Then decide which of the policies 1–3 Britain should follow in the 1920s and 1930s.

Concerns

1 The Empire was seen as crucial in order for Britain to remain a great power. Trade with the Empire was very important (Source **B**).
2 The British economy had suffered in the war, markets were lost and factories and machinery needed updating.
3 The need to spend less – the war had cost £7 million a day and Britain would be paying for it for a long time.
4 The need to improve living standards – which the Government had promised to do and would cost a great deal.
5 The need for peace because Britain depended on trade and this only prospered in peace time.

Source A A poster for the British Empire Exhibition

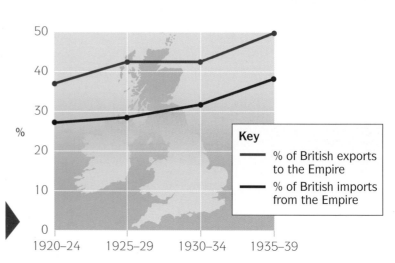

Source B Britain's trade with the Empire

Key
— % of British exports to the Empire
— % of British imports from the Empire

Problems

1 In 1920 the USA refused to join the League.
2 The conscripted soldiers in the Army had to be demobilised to avoid unrest or worse!
3 Growing nationalist movements in the Empire: Britain struggled to keep control of Ireland, Iraq, Egypt and India – this was very costly.
4 Germany, Russia, Italy and Japan were all unhappy with the Peace Treaties.
5 Britain and her Empire were increasingly vulnerable to new weapons, especially air attack. Her navy was threatened by the submarine.

Possible policies

Now decide which policy Britain should follow. To do this you need to satisfy as many concerns as possible and overcome as many problems as possible:

1 Disarm totally so you can put the money saved into improving living standards and the economy. Rely on the League of Nations to keep the peace.
2 Spend and defend – spend the money necessary to enforce the Peace Treaties and defend the Empire. This will mean not having the money to improve living standards at home, but if there is unrest you have the Army to deal with it.
3 Accept that Britain is vulnerable and do your best to avoid conflict and encourage disarmament. Germany, Italy and Japan have grievances, many of them are reasonable, so it is better to compromise and reach a fair settlement. This will mean accepting changes to the Peace Treaties. Rearm when Britain can afford it and as a last resort be prepared to fight.

The League was popular in Britain (Source **C**) but Britain was unable to work closely with France. Britain wanted Germany to recover her economic strength so they could trade, whereas France wanted to keep Germany permanently weak. Britain struggled to find the resources to act as a world power, she needed peace. So she followed policy 3. The name given to this policy was appeasement. It worked in the 1920s but in the 1930s the aggression of Italy, Japan and Nazi Germany meant this policy had to tackle more serious problems.

Source C Children at a League of Nations Union Rally in London, in 1921

Questions

1 **a)** What trend can you see in imports and exports between Britain and her Empire (Source **B**)?
   b) Can you think of a reason for this trend?

2 Write a full report explaining your choice of policy, include:
   i) the problems caused by the other two policies;
   ii) the advantage of your policy;
   iii) which problems and concerns will be overcome;
   iv) possible future problems.

3 Would Britain find it easy to support the collective security of the League?

The USA and isolationism

▶ Why did the USA reject the Treaty of Versailles and the League of Nations?

In 1919 the USA was the richest country in the world. It was also potentially the most powerful. The role it would play in international relations would be crucial. President Wilson had agreed to the Treaty of Versailles but the US Senate now had to ratify (agree to) the Treaty. The Senate was controlled by Wilson's opponents, the Republican Party, who opposed the Treaty and American involvement in the League of Nations (Source **A**). Many Americans thought the Treaty too harsh on Germany. The idea of the League was also unpopular. Others knew or cared little about Europe. Some Americans thought the League of Nations was a baseball league!

Source A 'Handle with Carelessness' a cartoon from the New York Tribune Newspaper. It shows the Senate throwing out Wilson's proposals.

Source B Should America ratify the Treaty and join the League?

YES
Wilson and his Democratic Party supporters

NO
The Republican Party and the majority of Americans

Yes – America has won the war and must stop Europe causing another war.

No – We do not agree with the harsh terms such as the War Guilt Clause and reparations.
- What about the cost? It will be the USA which ends up paying for the League.
- Britain and France will use the League to protect their Empires, America believes in self-determination and opposes Empires.
- Americans have just died in a pointless war in Europe, no more Americans should die sorting out other people's problems.
- Wilson never consulted the Senate before he went to Versailles, we cannot forgive this.

- America's business is business, not peace keeping. We do not want to stop selling goods to countries because of League sanctions (restrictions on trade).
- Europe means trouble, we are better off having nothing to do with it.

In March 1920 the Senate rejected the Treaty of Versailles. Then the leader of the Republicans, Warren Harding was elected President. There was now no chance of the USA changing its mind. At first the US government did not even open official mail from the League. Harding promised that America would concentrate on tackling its own problems and avoid those of Europe, this policy was known as isolationism.

In fact America did not return to total isolationism:
- The American Dawes Plan helped Europe with the problem of reparations (Source **C**). In 1924 an American bank loaned Germany $110 million.
- America signed the Kellogg-Briand Pact.
- America was concerned with events in South America and the Far East, and signed the Washington Naval Treaties.

But above all America did not want to become permanently involved with Europe and have to spend the money on an army and navy large enough to guarantee the peace in Europe. America was, however, keen to trade with other countries. In the 1920s the US flooded the world with American goods. She soon became the dominant economic power. But America was unwilling to import European products. This meant Europe could not earn the dollars to pay off American loans. So European nations struggled to recover from the war.

Source C   The American Plan. A cartoon from the San Francisco chronicle, January 1924.

Questions

1 Study Source **A**.
  a) How can you tell that the cartoonist supported Wilson from what is written on the boxes and barrels?
  b) The figure behind the tree is 'Uncle Sam' (America). What is his attitude to what is happening?

2 Study Source **C**. Even though American banks lent money to help Europe (the figures sitting in chairs), Americans were critical of Europe's failure to sort out the problem of reparations.
  a) Complete this sentence explaining America's attitude:
  'Dawes wanted Europe to face up to... by the use of... and...'
  b) How are the Europeans shown to be stuck in the past?
  c) From what you have read about war debts and reparations (pages 30-31), is this criticism of Europe fair?

3 Design two election posters, one supporting the Treaty of Versailles and American involvement in the League of Nations, the other opposing them.

Germany and the world 1919–29

What problems did Germany face?
When was Germany accepted again as an equal?

Problems at home and abroad

After the war Germany faced many problems. At home there were several attempts to overthrow the new Republic. First in 1919 Communists tried to seize power in Berlin and in Bavaria. Then in 1920 a right wing group tried to take control of Berlin. Finally in 1923 Adolf Hitler led a rebellion in Munich. All of these revolts failed. The new Republic had survived the political violence at home. Abroad it signed the Treaty of Rapallo with Russia in 1922 (see page 32).

The next major problem came with the French occupation of the Ruhr in 1923. This was a serious blow to the German economy, which collapsed under the strain. Prices rose sharply and the value of the German mark fell rapidly. By November 1923 a single match cost 900,000 marks and a bottle of beer cost 150,000,000,000 marks. (See Sources **A** and **B**.)

Source B From Egon Larsen, *Weimar Eyewitness*. Larsen was a journalist in Germany.

Bartering became more and more widespread. A haircut cost a couple of eggs, and craftsmen such as watchmakers displayed notices: 'Repairs carried out in exchange for food' … You went into a café and ordered a cup of coffee at the price shown, an hour later, when you asked for the bill, it had gone up by half or even double…

In August 1923 Gustav Stresemann became Chancellor. Then, in November, he was made Foreign Minister. Stresemann realised that Germany had to co-operate with its former enemies, and he ended passive resistance in the Ruhr.

Source A German bank note of 1923

Stability and the 'Spirit of Locarno'

In 1924 Germany began to stabilise and recover. French troops withdrew from the Ruhr. Germany accepted the Dawes Plan on reparations and a new currency replaced the worthless German mark. Then in 1925 a major step was taken to improve relations between Germany and her former enemies. At Locarno in Switzerland, Germany, Britain, Italy and Belgium met as equals to sign several treaties intended to make Europe a safer place (see page 32).

News of the Locarno Treaties was celebrated with church bells ringing and firework displays late into the night. It seemed that France had what she wanted, her border with Germany was guaranteed. Germany had accepted the terms of Versailles and had shown goodwill to France. People talked about a new spirit – the 'Spirit of Locarno' – which meant peace in Europe.

Source C From the diary of the British Ambassador in Germany

15 November 1925 It seems to me more difficult to exaggerate the importance of the Reparation Settlement in 1924 and the Treaty of Locarno in 1925.
10 January 1926 Another step forward. Germany has decided to send in her application for admission to the League of Nations.
2 October 1926 …The war spirit has been quelled, and the possibility of an era of peaceful development opens…the risk of war between France and Germany is vastly diminished.

Locarno – reassessed

Today historians point out that the problems in Europe had not been solved by Locarno.

1 Germany had already broken the Treaty of Versailles by her secret agreement in the Treaty of Rapallo with Russia which meant Germany was rearming.
2 Locarno did not deal with Germany's borders in the east with Poland and Czechoslovakia.
3 Locarno was seen as a great success for Stresemann. But he saw Locarno not as an acceptance of Versailles but as the first step to destroying it.
4 Many French people still felt insecure as France could now no longer invade Germany to enforce the Treaty of Versailles as she had done in 1923. Also they knew that allied troops would leave the Rhineland. Thus, France decided to build the Maginot Line.

5 Russia was not involved in the Locarno Treaties and was left feeling even more insecure.

Source D Comments from a modern historian, Sally Marks

The real spirit of Locarno behind the facade of public fellowship was one of bitter confrontation between a fearful France and a bitter Germany.

Most of the agreements made at Locarno were to be broken in the 1930s. But for a brief period Europe appeared to have achieved peace and harmony. The Dawes Plan seemed to have sorted out the problem of reparations and Locarno led to more American money being invested in Germany. Prosperity returned and Stresemann seemed to have returned Germany to peace and stability.

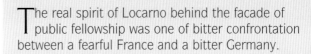

Questions

1 In January 1923 one US dollar bought 10,000 marks, by September it bought 98 million marks. Work out how many dollars the banknote (Source **A**) could buy in January 1923 and September 1923.

2 a) Which of the problems 1–5 not solved by Locarno would be of most concern in 1925 to:
   • France?
   • Britain?
  b) Which country in Europe would most fear Problem 1?

3 a) Study Source **D**. What reasons might still exist in 1924 for France to be 'fearful' and Germany to be 'bitter'?
  b) Do you think Sally Marks was correct – did such reasons still exist in 1925?
  c) If she is correct who posed a greater threat to peace in 1925 – a 'fearful France' or a 'bitter Germany'?

4 In pairs discuss who was least to be trusted in 1925 – Germany, France or Russia? Three important points to include in your discussions are below.
  • The Treaty of Rapallo broke the terms of Versailles.
  • Russia is Communist.
  • In 1923 France had used German failure to deliver some timber as a payment for reparations (a minor default) as a reason to occupy the Ruhr.

Russia and the world 1919–34

▶ *Why did Russia feel threatened?*
How did Russia's relations with other countries change?

Civil war

The Communist revolution of 1917 in Russia meant Russia became an outcast in Europe. To enable the revolution to succeed the new Russian leader, Lenin, made peace with Germany. This angered Russia's former allies, Britain, France, the USA and Japan. They sent troops to fight the Communists in the civil war which followed the revolution in Russia (Source **A**). By 1919 these forces had been defeated.

International Revolution

Lenin believed it was his duty to encourage Communist revolutions in other countries. Therefore, in 1919 he set up the Communist International (usually known as the Comintern) to help spread Communist ideas and plan revolutions. It soon became clear, however, that Russia was not strong enough to bring about a world Communist revolution. This was shown in 1920 when Poland attacked Russia. In March 1921 Russia had to agree to the Treaty of Riga, in which it lost territory to Poland.

Famine

Revolution and civil war had left Russia in ruins. A long drought caused a severe famine in 1921 and about five million people died. Some people turned to cannibalism and body snatching to survive (Sources **B** and **C**).

Source A Foreign troops help the white (anti-Communist) armies

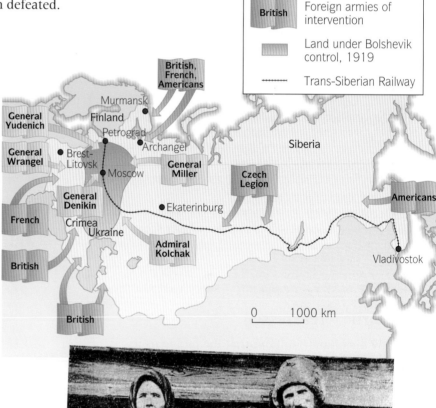

Key

General Denikin — White armies and their leaders

British — Foreign armies of intervention

— Land under Bolshevik control, 1919

······ Trans-Siberian Railway

British, French, Americans

Murmansk

General Yudenich

Finland

Petrograd

General Wrangel

Brest-Litovsk

Archangel

Moscow

General Miller

Siberia

Czech Legion

Americans

General Denikin

Ekaterinburg

French

Crimea

Ukraine

Admiral Kolchak

British

Vladivostok

0   1000 km

British

Source B A Russian doctor wrote:

Sometimes a starving family eats the body of one of its junior members… sometimes parents at night take part of a body from the cemetery and feed it to their children.

Source C Cannibals with their victims

Relations slowly improve

The Russian leaders realised they would have to come to terms with the major capitalist powers. They tried to persuade other countries to officially recognise the communist government and to trade with Russia. In April 1922 Russia signed the Treaty of Rapallo with Germany (see page 32). This brought German money and experts to Russia.

After 1922 relations with other countries improved, but Russia remained suspicious of the capitalist powers. The Russians believed these countries were planning to attack. Russia distrusted the League of Nations.

Lenin died in 1924. There was a long struggle for power, but by 1928 Stalin was ruler of Russia (Source **D**). He continued to improve relations with other countries, signing the Kellogg-Briand Pact in 1928 (see pages 32–33). He believed Russia should concentrate on building up its strength at home; it was not ready to lead a world revolution. So he used the Comintern, not for stirring up revolution, but for spying and spreading propaganda.

The 1930s – New threats to Russia

In the 1930s a new threat to Russia came from Japan and Hitler's Germany. Stalin tried to meet this threat by finding new allies, and in 1934 Russia joined the League of Nations. This change in Soviet foreign policy is explained in Source **E**, a modern Russian history book.

Source E From *History of Soviet Foreign Policy 1917–45*, Moscow, 1969

Naturally, the Soviet Union saw all the League's weaknesses, its hesitation in stopping aggression. Furthermore, it took into account the anti-Soviet trends in the League's past activities. But... the League could to some extent slow down the drift towards war, it could be used to expose and wreck the anti-Soviet aggressive plans.

World events in the 1930s and the rise of Fascism were to draw Russia more and more into European affairs and eventually into the Second World War.

Source D   Joseph Stalin

Profile

• Original name – Josef Djugashvili but he changed it to Stalin (man of steel).

• Born in 1879 in Georgia. His father, a shoemaker, abandoned the family when Stalin was a child. Stalin was expelled from school for spreading Communist ideas.

• He was exiled to Siberia and escaped six times. Played a major role in the 1917 Revolution and the Civil war.

• 1922 became General Secretary of the Communist Party. He was a good organiser. When Lenin died Stalin slowly eliminated his rivals and became leader of Russia.

• He ruled like a dictator and was ruthless, cunning and determined. His aim was to ensure Communist power by making Russia a powerful industrial state.

Questions

1 How does Source **A** help explain Communist Russia's fear of capitalist countries?

2 How might a Russian and an American textbook differ in explaining how the people in Source **C** came to be cannibals?

3 Lenin called the League of Nations 'a robber's den to safeguard the unjust spoils of Versailles'. What do you think he meant?

4 Source **E** gives one interpretation of why Russia joined the League of Nations. The author of this book gives a different explanation. Explain how they differ and why.

5 If you were an adviser to the Russian government, how would your advice on relations with the League of Nations change between these dates: 1919, 1928 and 1935?

Mussolini and Fascist Italy

▶ *How did Mussolini make Italy the first Fascist country in Europe?*
What were Mussolini's aims for Italy?

Italy's problems

Do you think you would make a good leader for your country? Why? What qualities do you think a good leader should have? Source **A** describes Benito Mussolini. Did he possess any of these qualities? Do you think he would be a good leader? He was asked to be Prime Minister of Italy in 1922.

Source A Profile of Benito Mussolini

▼

- Born 29 July 1883. Mother was a schoolteacher, Father a blacksmith.
- Expelled from school for wounding another boy and leading a protest against school food.
- Arrested several times for leading demonstrations.
- Qualified as a teacher and moved to Switzerland. Became interested in the Communist ideas of Karl Marx. Expelled from Switzerland for supporting revolutionary movements.
- In 1911 became editor of *Avanti!* (Forward!) the Socialist Party Newspaper. Changed his politics when Italy entered the First World War. He left the Socialist Party and set up his own newspaper *Il Popolo d'Italia* (The people of Italy).
- Joined the army and fought bravely. Wounded in 1917 and returned to edit his newspaper.
- Interested in politics, drink and women. Contracted VD. As a teacher admitted he could not keep order – bribed children with sweets to keep them quiet. An adventurer, a man of action – excited by new ideas, but often impatient and short-tempered.

Source C Italo Balbo, a Fascist leader, remembers how he and many other Italians felt at the time

▼

When I came back from the war I, like so many others, hated politics and politicians who, it seemed to me, had betrayed the hopes of the fighting men and had inflicted on Italy a shameful peace…

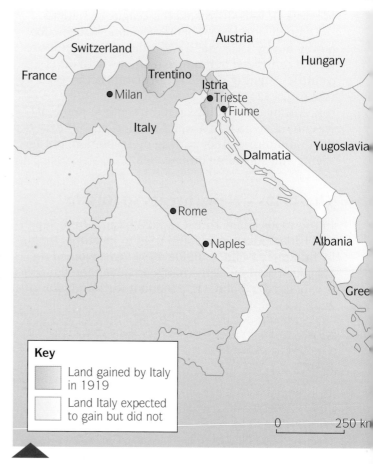

Key
- Land gained by Italy in 1919
- Land Italy expected to gain but did not

0   250 km

Source B Italy and the Peace Treaties

In 1919 King Victor Emmanuel III of Italy and his government faced major problems. The war had seriously damaged Italy's economy. Many soldiers could not get jobs when they returned from the war. Prices had risen by 500% since 1915, and there were many strikes and riots. The government was weak. MPs took bribes, and often behaved like unruly schoolchildren, fighting and throwing paper at each other.

Italy had entered the war on the side of the Allies, mainly because it was promised more territory at the end of the war. But in the Peace Treaties these promises were broken. Italy did not receive Dalmatia and Fiume as it had expected (Source **B**). Many Italians were shocked and angry with their Government and with the Allies (Source **C**).

Mussolini comes to power

Law and order began to break down. Such conditions were ripe for the growth of extreme parties. In opposition to the Communists, Benito Mussolini set up the extreme right-wing Fascist Party. He organised groups of supporters into fighting groups called Fasci di Combattimento, whose uniform was the black shirt.

The Fascists were ready to use violent methods against their opponents. Mussolini's 'blackshirt' Fasci groups attacked the meetings and buildings of Communists and Socialists. They forced some opponents to drink castor oil or eat live toads – others were beaten and killed. Between October 1920 and October 1922 the Fascists murdered an estimated 2,000 people.

In October 1922 the Fascists marched to Rome to seize power. King Victor Emmanuel was afraid of a civil war and worried he might lose his throne. So he invited Mussolini to become Prime Minister. Mussolini set about increasing his power and by 1927 he had many of the powers of a dictator.

Foreign Policy

Mussolini took the title 'Duce' (leader) and dreamed of building a new Roman Empire centred on the Mediterranean. He believed he needed to stir up a desire for war in the Italian people and he used slogans to do this (Source **D**).

Source E Benito Mussolini

Source D Mussolini's slogans

It is a crime not to be strong!
War is to men what childbearing is to women!
Nothing has ever been won in history without bloodshed!

In 1925 Mussolini signed the Locarno Treaty and in 1928 the Kellogg-Briand Pact. In both, the signing countries promised not to use force to solve international disputes. Mussolini signed not because he believed in the treaties but because he thought it would show that Italy was playing a vital role in world affairs.

In the early 1930s Mussolini appeared to be a vital ally for Britain and France against the growing power of Nazi Germany. He feared a German takeover of Austria, Italy's northern neighbour. In 1934 Mussolini warned Hitler that he would fight to protect Austria, and moved Italian troops up to the border. Hitler backed down. Leaders from Britain and France met Mussolini at Stresa, in Italy, and the three nations formed the 'Stresa Front' against the growing threat from Germany.

Questions

1 **a)** How did Mussolini's political views change between 1914 and 1919 (Source **A**)?
   b) Which country did Dalmatia become part of (Source **B**)?
   c) Which country was Mussolini most likely to regard as Italy's enemy (Source **B**)?

2 Are the slogans in Source **D** the words of a man of peace or an aggressive dictator?

3 Why did Britain and France regard Mussolini as a very useful ally by 1935?

Japan's problems

What problem did Japan face in the 1920s

The Far East

After the First World War Japan was the most powerful country in the Far East (Source **A**). Britain and France were important naval powers in the area.

Other countries included:
1 China – a decaying empire falling into chaos.
2 USSR – struggling to recover from the civil war.
3 Colonies of the European Powers such as Britain, France and the Netherlands.

Source A The Far East

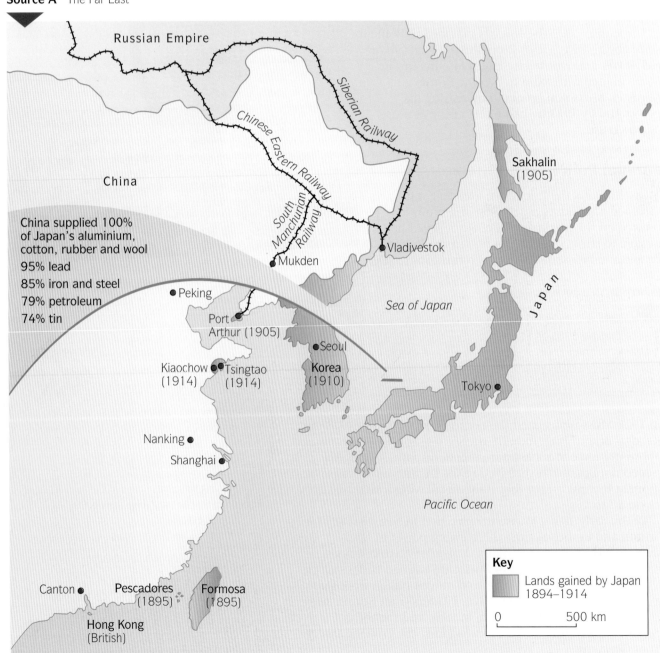

Russian Empire

Siberian Railway

Chinese Eastern Railway

South Manchurian Railway

Sakhalin (1905)

China

China supplied 100% of Japan's aluminium, cotton, rubber and wool
95% lead
85% iron and steel
79% petroleum
74% tin

Mukden

Vladivostok

Sea of Japan

Japan

Peking

Port Arthur (1905)

Seoul

Korea (1910)

Kiaochow (1914) Tsingtao (1914)

Tokyo

Nanking

Shanghai

Pacific Ocean

Canton

Pescadores (1895)

Formosa (1895)

Hong Kong (British)

Key

Lands gained by Japan 1894–1914

0   500 km

Problems abroad

Japan had been on the winning side in the First World War. But after 1919 relations with the western powers hit problems. These problems began with the Treaty of Versailles:

1 Japan wanted an empire. It had controlled Korea since 1905 but now looked eagerly at parts of China. At Versailles Japan had to fight hard to make gains. The USA resisted Japanese claims to the former German colonies in the area. Japan refused to leave the former German colony of Shantung in China which it had occupied in 1914, this was a defeat for President Wilson's idea of national self-determination. Japan resented Britain, the USA and France as she had not been given as many rewards at Versailles as she had expected (Source **B**).

Source B An American cartoon from 1919. The conductor is President Wilson at the Peace Conference at Versailles.

— Rear view —

2 Japan saw the Western Powers as a sort of 'white man's club' which dominated the Far East. It wanted to change this and include a clause in the covenant of the League of Nations stating that different races were equal. This was strongly opposed by the Australian Prime Minister who believed it would result in uncontrollable Japanese immigration to Australia. The clause was not accepted.

The USA was concerned about Japanese power in the Far East and in 1922 persuaded Japan to sign the Washington Treaty in an attempt to control the size of the navies of the great powers (see page 32). After this relations with the USA slowly became worse. In 1924 the USA stopped Asians emigrating to the USA, Japan deeply resented this and felt insulted.

Problems at home

Japan also faced serious problems at home which affected her relations with other countries. She did not have the raw materials she needed, such as iron-ore, oil, rubber and timber. Nor could she grow enough food to feed her population. So she imported what she needed from China and exported silk to pay for them. When world trade slumped in the Depression which began at the end of 1929, Japan was hit hard. The demand for silk fell sharply and the value of Japan's exports fell by nearly 50%. Japan could no longer afford to buy all the food and raw materials she needed.

The Japanese government faced another problem, they had difficulty controlling the power of the army and the Zaibatsu (large industrial companies). Army leaders believed the answer to Japan's problems was in China. Since 1905 Japan had controlled Korea. It also owned the South Manchurian Railway which was vital in supplying the food and raw materials needed. To safeguard these the Army wanted to expand Japan's empire by invading Manchuria. This would bring Japan into conflict not only with China but also with the League of Nations.

Questions

1 In Source **B** there is a contradiction between the song title and the items sticking out of the back pockets, explain this contradiction in the case of Japan.

2 Prepare a report for the Japanese government advising how best to solve these problems:
   a) more land for its growing population;
   b) safeguarding the imports of raw materials and food;
   c) safeguarding the South Manchurian Railway which it built and controlled;
   d) more markets for its industrial goods;
   e) stopping what it saw as racial insults from the western powers.

5 Keeping the peace

The League of Nations

▶ **What were the League's aims? How did the League work?
What were the League's strengths and weaknesses?**

Before you read further, discuss what you think 'collective security' means.

Before 1914 the Great Powers had split into two alliances which seemed to balance each other out. Neither side could be sure of winning a war, so they would not provoke one. But this idea failed and by 1919 the balance of power was gone. The death and destruction of the war led people to look for a new way of keeping world peace. President Wilson proposed an international organisation called the League of Nations which would solve disputes between countries in a peaceful way. The idea was that all members would agree to protect each other against an aggressor. This idea was known as 'collective security'. If two members were in dispute then the League would decide who was in the wrong and would enforce that decision. League members would be secure as together they would be too powerful for any single country.

Aims and organisation

The aims and organisation of the League were set out in the Covenant, this was a solemn promise signed by all members. (Sources **A** and **B**.) The Covenant was also included in all of the peace treaties. The League began work in 1920. Its headquarters were in Geneva in Switzerland.

Source A The aims of the League

> **1** To keep world peace by dealing with disputes between nations.
> **2** To safeguard the independence of countries and their new frontiers.
> **3** To encourage nations to reduce their armaments.
> **4** To improve living and working conditions for all people.

THE COUNCIL

Consisted of four permanent members (Britain, France, Italy, Japan) and non-permanent members (at first four and later seven). It met on average five times a year and to deal with emergencies. For action to be taken all members had to agree. Each permanent member had a veto – the right to stop the Council taking action.

THE ASSEMBLY

Every member sent representatives and had one vote. It met at least once a year. It could recommend action to the Council and could:
• discuss any matter raised by a member;
• fix the League's budget;
• admit new members;
• elect the non-permanent members of the Council.
A unanimous vote was needed for a decision.

Source B The organisation of the League

THE SECRETARIAT

An international civil service which prepared reports, kept records and translated documents.

THE PERMANENT COURT OF INTERNATIONAL JUSTICE

Set up in 1921 at The Hague, Holland. Fifteen judges gave a decision on disputes between countries – but only when the countries requested this.

COMMISSIONS AND AGENCIES

A wide range of agencies and commissions set up to deal with various problems.

INTERNATIONAL LABOUR ORGANISATION (ILO)

Tried to improve working conditions and wages.

MANDATES COMMISSION

The colonies of Germany and Turkey were given to 'caretaker' countries. The Commission kept an eye on how these colonies (mandates) were run.

MINORITIES COMMISSION

Helped protect people of one nationality forced to live under the rule of a different national group.

OTHER AGENCIES

These dealt with other problems such as drug abuse and improving world health and education. They included: Refugees Committee, Slavery Commission, Health Committee.

Questions

1 Study Source **B**. Which parts of the League's organisation would deal with:
   a) The League's main aim of keeping world peace?
   b) A request to join the League?
   c) Reports of slavery?
   d) Two countries both claiming ownership to a group of islands?
   e) A complaint about the way France was running Syria (a French mandate)?

The powers of the League

The hope was that disputes between members would be sorted out by discussion in the Council. If this failed the Council would decide which country was in the wrong and use the following powers against it:

1st Moral condemnation – condemn the actions of the country and tell it to stop.
2nd Economic sanctions – tell other countries not to trade with the country.
3rd Military force – use armed forces from member countries.

Strengths and weaknesses

In 1920 the League had a number of strengths and weaknesses:

Strengths

1 Forty four nations, including Britain, France, Italy and Japan joined.
2 Members wanted to co-operate and prevent any more wars.
3 Many people around the world supported the aims of the League.
4 The League had some powerful weapons, especially economic sanctions.
5 As a way of keeping the peace, the League was a step forward from the old alliance system.

Weaknesses

1 The Council was dominated by powerful European countries and appeared to others as too much of a 'European club'.
2 The most powerful country, the USA, refused to join. Other countries belonged only for short periods (Source **C**).
3 The League was tied into the Peace Treaties which some countries, for example Germany, were hostile to.
4 The League had no military force of its own.
5 For the League to act, unanimous votes were needed in the Council and Assembly (excluding those in the dispute).

Source C Membership of the League – the Great Powers

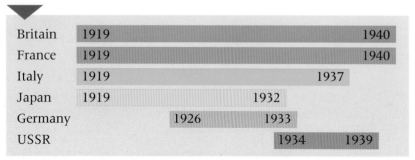

Britain	1919	1940
France	1919	1940
Italy	1919	1937
Japan	1919	1932
Germany	1926	1933
USSR	1934	1939

Chances of success

Now you have studied how the League worked and its strengths and weaknesses, look at the following possible problems and decide how successful the League was likely to be.

First decide what action the League should take i.e. which country is in the wrong and which powers the League should use.

Secondly, decide how likely this action was to succeed, use a scale of 1–5, 1 is immediate failure, 5 is total and immediate success. Remember Britain and France are the two leading members and the USA is not a member.

Problem 5

Japan, a powerful Far Eastern country, has invaded a weaker neighbour China. China appeals to the League.

Problem 1

Two small and not very powerful countries (Sweden and Finland) both claim some nearby islands. The islands are controlled by Finland but most of the population is from Sweden.

Problem 2

Two countries Poland and Lithuania quarrel over ownership of a city with a mixed population. The Peace Treaties gave the city to Lithuania but Poland has taken it by force. Lithuania appeals to the League.

Problem 3

Some soldiers from Italy (a powerful and permanent member of the Council of the League) are killed by bandits when they are helping map the border between Albania and Greece. Therefore Italy demands compensation from Greece as the bandits came from Greece. Then Greece asks the League to investigate but Italy says it is nothing to do with the League and invades an island belonging to Greece.

Questions

1 Look at the problems surrounding the world map. Which is the easiest problem to solve?

2 Which is the most difficult problem to solve?

3 What particular problem would leading members of the League, Britain and France, have in dealing with Problem 5?

4 Would your decisions on how likely the League was to succeed have differed if the USA had been a member?

5 Which problem would the USA have been especially helpful in solving?

6 From what you have learnt so far, do you think the League will be successful?

Problem 4

The powerful European state Italy has invaded the weak African state Abyssinia which appeals to the League for help. Italy is a member of the Council and the main ally of Britain and France against the rising power of Nazi Germany. If it can be avoided, Britain and France do not want to lose Italy as an ally.

The work of the League in the 1920s

▶ *How successful was the League in the 1920s?*

In the 1920s there was plenty of work for the League to do in helping clear up the chaos left by the war. The League helped return 400,000 prisoners of war to their own countries and found homes for countless refugees (Source **A**). Other problems the League tackled included the growing traffic in dangerous drugs, the illegal sale of weapons, the sale of women and children as slaves, and the spread of disease. For example in the British colony of Sierra Leone it helped free 200,000 slaves. The League also helped raise loans to save Austria and Hungary from bankruptcy.

There were also many disputes about new borders. Some of these disputes were settled by a Conference of Ambassadors set up to ensure the decisions of the Peace Conference were carried out. Sometimes there was confusion over whether the League or the conference should sort out a problem. The League had both successes and failures in settling disputes and problems. Source **B** shows the disputes and problems tackled by the League in the 1920s. Study each of these and decide if it was a success or a failure for the League.

Source A The Opera House in Athens was transformed into living quarters for homeless Greek families

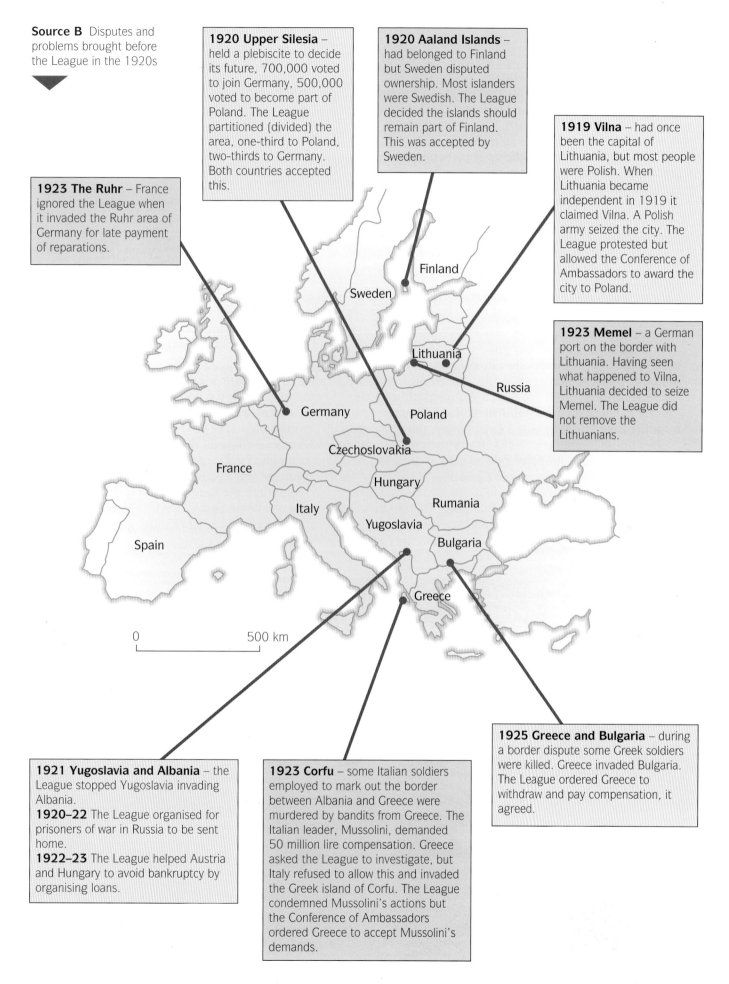

Source B Disputes and problems brought before the League in the 1920s

1920 Upper Silesia – held a plebiscite to decide its future, 700,000 voted to join Germany, 500,000 voted to become part of Poland. The League partitioned (divided) the area, one-third to Poland, two-thirds to Germany. Both countries accepted this.

1920 Aaland Islands – had belonged to Finland but Sweden disputed ownership. Most islanders were Swedish. The League decided the islands should remain part of Finland. This was accepted by Sweden.

1919 Vilna – had once been the capital of Lithuania, but most people were Polish. When Lithuania became independent in 1919 it claimed Vilna. A Polish army seized the city. The League protested but allowed the Conference of Ambassadors to award the city to Poland.

1923 The Ruhr – France ignored the League when it invaded the Ruhr area of Germany for late payment of reparations.

1923 Memel – a German port on the border with Lithuania. Having seen what happened to Vilna, Lithuania decided to seize Memel. The League did not remove the Lithuanians.

1921 Yugoslavia and Albania – the League stopped Yugoslavia invading Albania.
1920–22 The League organised for prisoners of war in Russia to be sent home.
1922–23 The League helped Austria and Hungary to avoid bankruptcy by organising loans.

1923 Corfu – some Italian soldiers employed to mark out the border between Albania and Greece were murdered by bandits from Greece. The Italian leader, Mussolini, demanded 50 million lire compensation. Greece asked the League to investigate, but Italy refused to allow this and invaded the Greek island of Corfu. The League condemned Mussolini's actions but the Conference of Ambassadors ordered Greece to accept Mussolini's demands.

1925 Greece and Bulgaria – during a border dispute some Greek soldiers were killed. Greece invaded Bulgaria. The League ordered Greece to withdraw and pay compensation, it agreed.

0   500 km

You may have realised that the 'problems' 1–3 you considered on pages 50–51 are real problems shown in Source **B**. Match them up and check to see if your decisions were the same as the League's. Were you correct on the chances of success?

The League was usually successful when a dispute occurred between small, weak countries. However, when a dispute involved a great power, the League often favoured the more important country. The Council of the League dealt with emergencies and the great powers dominated the Council.

Two of the incidents in Source **B** show how the League failed to treat the great powers and the small countries equally: the Corfu incident in 1923 and the dispute between Greece and Bulgaria in 1925. Both incidents involved Greece, the events were very similar but the outcome was different.

In the Corfu incident Italy pushed the League aside and used force to get compensation from Greece for the murder of Italian soldiers. But when, in the second dispute, Greece tried to use force, it did not receive compensation for the murder of Greek soldiers but instead had to pay for invading Bulgaria. Italy was a great power; the other great powers in the League were anxious not to upset the Italians (Source **C**). Greece, however, was a small, weak country with no powerful friends on the Council.

The Corfu incident was seen as a serious failure for the League in the 1920s. It showed that powerful nations could still bully a less powerful neighbour (Source **D**).

Source D   An historian, G. Scott, writing in 1973

The settlement made a nasty smell. The Greeks were bitter, the Assembly felt it had been betrayed and that the League had been degraded. Mussolini appeared to have triumphed in his assertion that where a nation was powerful enough it was justified in using force to further its interests and the League had no right to interfere.

The Geneva Protocol

In 1924 the British Prime Minister, Ramsey Macdonald, drafted the Geneva Protocol in an attempt to strengthen the League. This said that if the League made a decision in a dispute then the countries involved would have to accept it. But Macdonald fell from power later that year and the new Government, together with many other countries, refused to sign the Protocol. They did not like the idea of being compelled to accept the League's decisions. The Protocol was abandoned. It had been meant to strengthen the League, but it only showed up the weakness of the League – that countries could refuse to accept the League's decisions.

Source C   A British cartoon comments on Mussolini's use of force in the Corfu incident

Source E The Devil's Toyshop. The boy figures represent France, Britain, the USA and Italy (Mussolini is at the front). They have come to spend their pocket money on the 'toys' which fascinate them.

Disarmament

As well as safeguarding the peace the other main aim of the League was to encourage countries to disarm. The League tried to persuade countries to disarm but failed. By the end of the 1920s countries were beginning to rearm (Source **E**). The League also failed to stop the trade in armaments. Again its weakness when dealing with the Great Powers is shown by an incident in 1928. At a border post on the border of Austria and Hungary railway trucks carrying cases labelled MACHINE PARTS were waiting to cross the border. Unusually they were opened and checked by customs men. Sixty tons of machine gun parts were discovered. They had come from Italy but the League failed to even ask Mussolini for an explanation. Britain and France did not want to upset Italy and other smaller nations were afraid to ask. The League merely issued a general warning about arms smuggling.

Questions

1 **a)** What possessions can you see in Source **A** on page 52?
   b) What do you think the buckets were for?

2 Study Source **C**.
   a) How are most of the League members reacting to the use of force?
   b) What has happened to the League's peace plans?
   c) Which League member is smiling? What reason would that country have for being pleased?
   d) Is this cartoon an accurate comment on the League's behaviour?

3 What does G. Scott mean by 'the settlement made a nasty smell' (Source **D**)?

4 Study Source **E**.
   a) What 'toys' can you see?
   b) Do you think the cartoonist, David Low, saw the leader as sensible, wicked or just weak?
   c) How is Mussolini's attitude different to the other boys?
   d) Which events support Mussolini's attitude to weapons shown in the cartoon?

The Great Depression – Causes and consequences

▶ **Why was there a World Depression?**
How did International Relations suffer?

World trade

It is almost certain that since you woke up this morning you have made use of something made in another country – perhaps a radio, a car, pens, books, clothes or food. International trade is vital for every country. If that trade collapses, unemployment will rise rapidly. That is what happened in the early 1930s, in the Great Depression. Millions of people were affected.

Causes of the Depression

The origins of the Depression lay in the chaos caused by the First World War. In the 1920s the USA lent large sums of money to other countries to help them recover from the war. She lent most to Germany. The loans helped countries to buy and sell goods and thus helped trade to recover. However, many countries, while keen to sell goods abroad, tried to protect their own industries by putting up tariff barriers (taxes on imports). This is called protectionism.

The USA was the greatest trading nation on earth. In 1930 the USA also raised taxes on imported goods. This made it difficult to sell goods to America and so world trade suffered badly.

The other great problem was that world prices for agricultural goods such as coffee, wheat and sugar fell steadily during the 1920s. Whatever farmers produced, they all faced the same problem (Source A).

Source A From a hearing on unemployment in the US

> One American farmer told me he had killed 3,000 sheep this fall (Autumn) and thrown them down the canyon because it cost $1.10 to ship a sheep (to market) and then he would get less than a dollar for it. He said he could not afford to feed the sheep… so he just cut their throats.

Low prices meant that countries such as Brazil and Argentina, which depended on selling agricultural goods, could buy little from industrialised countries such as the USA and Britain.

The Wall Street Crash

By the late 1920s world trade was in difficulty. Then, in 1929, the American stock market (centred on Wall Street, in New York) crashed. American banks wanted countries to repay the money they had lent them. This hit Europe badly. Banks and factories closed. Soon there was a world-wide economic slump (Source **B**).

Source B Percentage decline in the value of imports and exports, 1929–31

	Imports
USA, Germany	over 50 %
Italy, Austria	over 40 %
Great Britain, France	over 25 %

	Exports
Cuba	over 70 %
Brazil	over 60 %
Argentina	over 65 %
USA	over 50 %
Great Britain, Austria	over 40 %
France, Italy	over 30 %
Germany	over 25 %
Russia	under 15 %

Unemployment

Millions lost their jobs as industries were ruined (Source **C**). In many countries the unemployed received little or no help from the government. Many people went hungry (Source **D**).

A World Economic Conference, set up to find a solution, collapsed in 1933.

Source C Unemployment in millions

	USA	Germany	Britain
1929	1.55	2.48	1.20
1932	12.06	6.12	2.80

Source D The wife and children of an agricultural worker in the USA in the mid 1930s

Source E One French woman, Morvan Lebesque, later wrote of her experience

I spent the winter of 1923 on the streets, it snowed and froze, thousands of young men, forced out of their jobs by the crisis, struggled on to their last penny, to the end of their tether then, in despair, abandoned the fight. On the street benches and at tube stations groups of exhausted and starving young men would be trying not to die… I saw a child drop a sweet which someone trod on, then the man behind bent down and picked it up, wiped it and ate it.

International Relations suffer

The Depression was a turning point. Trade between countries encourages those countries to be on good terms. When trade suffers then relations often suffer, this happened in the 1930s. Some countries tried to solve their economic problems by invading neighbours. Other countries wanted to concentrate on solving problems at home rather than international problems. Therefore, the League of Nations was faced with major problems to solve at the very time that the will of its members to keep the peace by working together was weakened (Source **F**).

Source F The Depression and International Relations

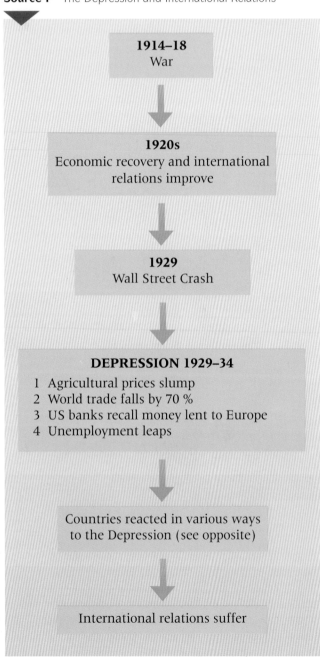

1914–18
War

↓

1920s
Economic recovery and international relations improve

↓

1929
Wall Street Crash

↓

DEPRESSION 1929–34
1 Agricultural prices slump
2 World trade falls by 70 %
3 US banks recall money lent to Europe
4 Unemployment leaps

↓

Countries reacted in various ways to the Depression (see opposite)

↓

International relations suffer

Countries reacted in various ways to the Depression:

Germany – mass unemployment made people disillusioned with the Weimer Republic. The Nazis came to power and promised to overturn the Treaty of Versailles. German rearmament speeded up.

Japan – 50% of Japan's heavy industry closed, the vital silk export trade was destroyed. These economic problems strengthened the hand of the army which wanted to find new markets and raw materials by invading Japan's neighbours.

Italy – Mussolini wanted to distract attention from economic problems by enlarging the Italian Empire in Africa.

USA – retreated further into isolation.

Britain – concentrated on economic problems at home and delayed rearming as it feared this would further harm its economy.

France – internal political problems made France delay rearmament.

USSR – the Depression had little effect on Russia which had few trade links with the rest of the world.

These changes in individual countries led to a number of international problems. Here are seven such problems, try and match each one to a country above. For example the actions of Japan led to problem one.

Problems

1 Invading China would upset the League of Nations, but what could the League do? Europe was a long way away.
2 The most powerful country in the world turned its back on international problems and concentrated on rebuilding its economy.
3 The collapse of world trade suggested that capitalism was wrong and communism was right, so this country was even more suspicious of capitalist countries.
4 With other countries worried about their problems at home, here was the chance to tear up the Treaty of Versailles and retake lost territory.
5 Unemployment caused this country to delay rearmament, but when the threat from its neighbour increased it built a massive line of forts along its border.
6 Relations with other democracies suffered and this country wanted to work with its great Empire and avoid conflict which might threaten its Empire.
7 Invading Abyssinia, an independent African country, would upset the League and could mean the loss of Britain and France as allies. There was always Germany to ally with.

So the Depression helped cause international problems and make relations between countries more difficult. Recovery was going to take a long time (Source **G**). The following pages look in detail at some of the consequences of the Depression. First, how it led to the rise of the Nazis in Germany whose ideas pushed Europe into war. Then how it caused the Japanese invasion of China. Finally, how it brought about the Italian invasion of Abyssinia which forced Italy to resign from the League and ally with Germany.

Source G   A British cartoon of 1931 sums up the European view that war debts still owed to the USA were hindering recovery from the Depression

Questions

1 Study Sources **B** and **C** on pages 56–57.
   a) Which country suffered the largest rise in unemployment?
   b) Which three exporting countries do you think exported mainly agricultural products?
   c) Which countries suffered a greater decline in imports than in exports?

2 Who might the woman in Source **D** on page 57 blame for her family's poverty?

3 a) What attitude towards America is shown in Source **G**?
   b) Which countries are suffering most from the effects of war debts?

4 Why were nations very reluctant to use the League's most powerful weapon of economic sanctions?

5 One historian has called the Depression 'the third global catastrophe of the century'. What do you think the other two catastrophes were? How can the Depression be seen as a global catastrophe?

6 How do you rate the chances of the League in 1933 keeping the peace through collective security?

Germany in the Depression

How did the Depression help the Nazis?
What did the Nazis promise? What were Nazi beliefs?

The Depression hits Germany

By 1928 the German economy seemed to have fully recovered from the war. In the election of 1928 the National Socialist (Nazi) Party was a small right wing party which only won 2.6% of the vote. It was one of the many small extremist parties and was not taken very seriously by most people. Yet in less than five years its leader, Adolf Hitler, was Chancellor of Germany. This was a remarkable turnabout. The key reason was the Depression, which the Nazis took advantage of more than anyone. The Depression hit Germany very hard, the main stages were:

1 Agricultural prices fell, this brought poverty to the countryside. The Nazis appealed to the farmers, many of them listened to the Nazi message.
2 The Wall Street Crash led to the withdrawal of US loans. This hit Germany worse than other countries. Also, Gustav Stresemann, the man who had led Germany to recovery, died. Unemployment rose to 5.5 million in 1931. Many of the unemployed were now ready to listen to extremists such as the Nazis and Communists (Source **A**).
3 In 1931 the five major banks in Germany crashed. This meant many businesses failed and many middle class people lost their savings. These people were also now ready to listen to the Nazi message.
4 Big businesses were worried because the Communist vote had also increased. They preferred the unemployed to support the Nazis rather than the Communists. They put pressure on President Hindenburg to allow Hitler to join the Government.

Source A Egon Larsen, *Weimar Eyewitness*. Larsen was a journalist at the time in Germany.

The life of a young jobless worker was often intolerable. On dole days he had to join an endless queue outside his labour exchange (job centre) waiting for hours for his turn... those political organisations (Nazis and Communists) offered him some kind of social life at the end of the day, a uniform which made him feel important, and perhaps a plate of soup or a sandwich. The evening usually began with a get-together and a pep talk by some propaganda officer at the local headquarters – the backroom of a pub – and the men went on a 'patrol' of the district, looking for trouble. (Source **G**.)

Hitler becomes Chancellor

These events caused the Nazi vote to increase dramatically (Sources **B** and **C**). In July 1932 the Nazi Party was the largest party in the German Parliament – the Reichstag (Source **D**). But in the November 1932 election the Nazi vote dropped back. There then followed a power struggle in the German Government which ended in the President asking Hitler to become Chancellor. It was believed that Hitler and the Nazis could be controlled by other experienced politicians. However, Hitler quickly called another election. Just before the election the Reichstag Building was set on fire. Hitler cleverly blamed the Communists, the Nazis vote increased. By 1934 Hitler had banned other political parties and was creating a Nazi dictatorship. The Depression and the unemployment and poverty it caused were crucial to the change in Nazi fortunes.

Source B
Unemployment and the Nazi vote 1928–33

	Seats in the Reichstag	% of the vote	Unemployment
1928	12	2.6	1,391,000
1930	107	18.3	3,076,000
July 1932	230	37.3	5,603,000
November 1932	196	33.1	–
1933	288	43.9	4,804,000

Source C Unemployed Germans queue in 1932 for newspapers with job vacancies

Unemployment

This account is only a brief overview of the Nazi rise to power. Much of the detail is omitted, yet detail is very important in showing why people stopped supporting the other parties and started listening to Nazi promises. One such detail is unemployment pay.

In 1927 people could receive one of the three types of unemployment benefit:

1 Regular full benefit – from central government.
2 Crisis benefit   – from central government.
3 Local benefit   – paid by local government.

In 1930–31 the Government cut the first two benefits and pushed the responsibility for paying the unemployed onto the local council. For example, in the city of Cologne the cost rose to 4.3 million Reichmarks and the city faced bankruptcy. As the number of unemployed rose many towns and cities could not afford to keep paying unemployment benefit. Communists and Social Democrats had been elected to run many of these towns and cities and they took the blame for failing to pay benefits. Popular support for these councils now melted away, much of it turned to supporting the Nazis who were seen to be helping the unemployed by running soup kitchens and promising them work.

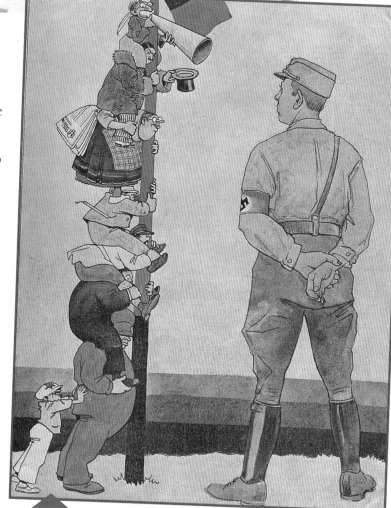

Source D Nazis a match for all other parties put together

The Nazi message

The Weimar Republic appeared to have no idea how to tackle the problems caused by the Depression. The Nazis, on the other hand, promised to solve the problems (Source **E**). Hitler promised most groups in Germany what they wanted:

Farmers	– higher prices for their produce.
Unemployed workers	– jobs building public works such as roads and stadiums.
Middle class	– to restore the profits of small businesses and the value of savings, and to end the Communist threat.

To all Germans he promised to restore German honour by tearing up the Treaty of Versailles and by making Germany great again.

Nazi beliefs

Behind these promises were a set of beliefs that were to lead to the Second World War and the death of millions of people:

1 Rearm Germany and retake what was lost at Versailles.
2 The German race (blonde blue eyed Aryans) were racially superior. But there were other minority races in Germany who had weakened Germany, they must be removed for Germany to become racially pure. Hitler called Germans the 'master race' (Sources **F** and **G**).
3 Racially pure Germans would work for the benefit of Germany. The state would come first, the citizen second. Germany would become a totalitarian state with a strong leader (Hitler and the Nazis would control all aspects of life).
4 The 'master race' needed more land, Hitler called it Lebensraum (living space). He looked eastwards at Poland and Russia whose 'inferior' races would work for the 'master race'.

Source E A Nazi election poster in 1928

NATIONAL SOZIALIST

ODER UMSONST WAREN DIE OPFER

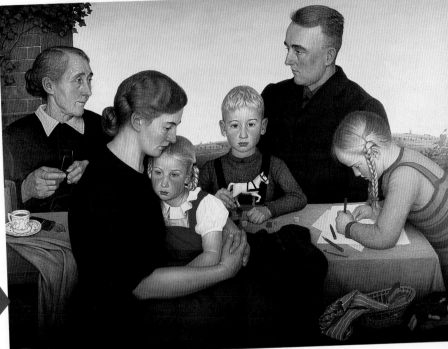

Source F An Aryan family

What we must fight for is to safeguard the existence and reproduction of our race… the purity of our blood and the independence of the fatherland, so that our people may achieve the mission given it by the creator of the universe.

Source H Adolf Hitler

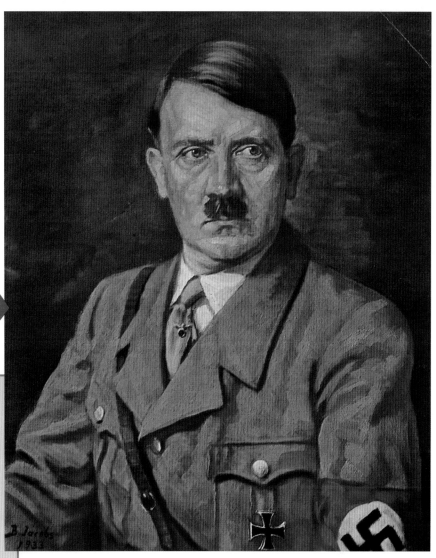

Profile of Hitler

Born in 1889 in Austria. His father was a customs official, the family name was originally Schickelgruber.

Hitler went to Vienna to fulfil his ambition of becoming an artist. He failed to win a scholarship and became an architect's draftsman. In Vienna he developed his hatred of foreigners and Jews.

In 1914 he joined the German Army. He was promoted to corporal and won the Iron Cross.

After the war he joined the German Workers Party in Munich and transformed it into the Nazi Party. In 1923 he led an attempt to overthrow the Bavarian Government but this failed. For this he spent nine months in prison where he dictated his book *Mein Kampf* (My Struggle).

After 1925 he rebuilt the Nazi Party. He became Chancellor in 1933 and President in 1934 and used the title Der Fuhrer – leader.

He led Germany to war in 1939 and tried to exterminate the Jews and other groups in Germany. When Germany was defeated in 1945 Hitler married his mistress Eva Braun in his bomb proof bunker in Berlin and shot himself on 30 April.

Questions

1 According to Egon Larsen in Source **A**, why did so many unemployed people join extreme political parties?

2 Using Source **B**, at which election do you think the Nazis made the decisive breakthrough?

3 Are the people in Source **F** pure Aryan Germans? How can you tell?

4 In Source **G** Hitler talks of his people's mission, what did he believe this to be?

5 **a)** If you had been able to ask Hitler his views about the following in 1932, what might he have said?
   • the Jews
   • the Treaty of Versailles
   • unemployment
   • the future of Germany.
   b) Which of the Nazi beliefs was most likely to be a threat to international peace?

6 The League of Nations in the 1930s

Japan and the League

▶ *How did the League deal with the Japanese invasion of Manchuria?*
Why did the League fail?

The League in the 1930s

In the 1930s the League faced more serious problems than it had in the 1920s. The Depression meant some countries were looking to expand overseas to solve economic problems at home. In 1930 all the major powers except for the USA and USSR were members of the League. But by 1936 Japan, Italy and Germany had all left and the idea of collective security was dead. The first serious challenge to the League in the 1930s came from Japan.

Japan invades Manchuria

To solve Japan's economic problems the army decided to invade Manchuria which was part of China (see page 47). Japan used her ownership of the South Manchurian Railway as an excuse. In September 1931 an explosion slightly damaged the railway line (Source **A**). The Japanese blamed the Chinese but the Japanese Army had faked the incident to give them the excuse to invade. They quickly took control of Manchuria. China appealed to the League (Source **B**).

The League sent a commission led by Lord Lytton to investigate the problem. The Japanese made it difficult for Lord Lytton to interview Chinese witnesses. Eight men who tried to speak to Lord Lytton were tortured and then murdered. Others sent information secretly to Lytton wrapped in bath towels, written on menus and hidden in cakes. Finally in November 1932 the Lytton report condemned the Japanese invasion. Japan had already announced that Manchuria was an independent state and renamed it Manchukuo. In fact it was run by the Japanese Army. Japan rejected the report and left the League.

The League fails to act

The League took no further action. The Lytton report did not recommend the use of economic sanctions or force against Japan. The League did not have the power or the will to act against Japan. Source **C** explains why.

Source A A Japanese photograph of the damage to the railway

Source B Chiang Kai-shek, the Chinese Leader

The challenge thrown to us is also a challenge to all nations. The League of Nations was established to prevent war and bring collective action into play to stop aggression. We have immediately... asked the League to obtain as a first step the immediate withdrawal of the invaders.

Source C How countries responded to Japan's invasion of Manchuria

Non members

USA – Believed in isolationism. Also because of the Depression she would not support the idea of trade sanctions.

USSR – Worried by a Japanese army on her border. But problems at home and no allies abroad meant she was not ready to act against Japan.

Members

Germany and Italy – Neither was interested in the Far East. They believed that like themselves Japan had real grievances and wanted to see if she would get away with the use of force.

Britain – Was not strong enough to stop Japan. Also parts of her Empire such as Hong Kong, Singapore and India could be in danger if war broke out.

France – Preoccupied with the need to protect her border with Germany. She did not want to endanger her Empire in South East Asia. Sympathised with Japan.

Other factors

1 The Depression – The fall in world trade meant that countries were preoccupied with unemployment problems at home. Nor did they want to endanger their trade with Japan and make things worse.
2 Japanese grievances – most powers agreed with the British view in Source **D**.

Therefore, the League failed in Manchuria. Only Britain and the USA had any military power in the region. Only Britain was a member of the League but she no longer had the power to act as the world's police officer without the support of other powers.

But perhaps the failure was not that serious (except for the Chinese). The affair had shown that if a powerful country far from Europe decided to ignore the League then it could do so. If the League was to suffer a similar failure in or near Europe then it could be much more serious.

Source E 'Tut, tut, Japsy, you should warn Auntie the next time you want to start a little war.'

Source D   Sir John Simon, British Foreign Secretary, 1931

There is a widespread feeling, which I believe to be justified, that although Japan had taken the law into her own hands and broken the Covenant of the League, she has a real grievance against China… Japanese lives and property in Manchuria have been attacked by Chinese bandits.

1 Study Source **A**.
  a) Do the rails or sleepers appear to be damaged?
  b) Would the track be easy or difficult to repair?
  c) Does this photograph help prove the Japanese blew up the railway?

2 What did Chiang Kai-shek mean in the first sentence of Source **B**?

3 What does the cartoonist think of the way the League tackled Japan (Source **E**)? How can you tell?

4 What grievances did Germany and Italy have that meant they were interested to see if Japan got away with the use of force?

5 Explain why the League failed to stop Japan. Include a political cause, an economic cause and a military cause.

Abyssinia and the League

▶ *Why did Italy invade Abyssinia?*
What were the consequences for the League of Nations?

Italy invades Abyssinia

The League did suffer a much more serious failure near Europe in 1936 when Italy invaded Abyssinia (modern Ethiopia). The Italian dictator, Mussolini, wanted to fight a war and create a great empire in the Mediterranean. He hoped to win the coal, iron, steel and oil Italy lacked, and distract Italians from problems in Italy. Mussolini also wanted to revenge a defeat by Abyssinia at the Battle of Adowa in 1896.

Abyssinia was sandwiched between the Italian colonies of Eritrea and Italian Somaliland (Source **A**). It was an independent country ruled by the Emperor Haile Selassie. As a member of the League of Nations it was one of the small countries which collective security was meant to protect.

Source A Italy and Abyssinia 1934–36

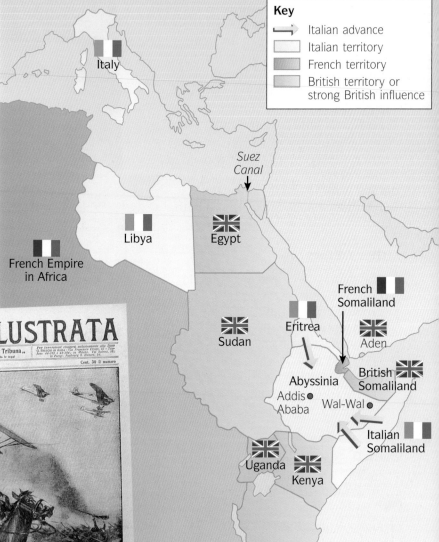

Key
- ➡ Italian advance
- ☐ Italian territory
- ☐ French territory
- ☐ British territory or strong British influence

Italy

Suez Canal

French Empire in Africa

Libya

Egypt

Sudan

Eritrea

French Somaliland

Aden

Abyssinia
Addis Ababa   Wal-Wal

British Somaliland

Italian Somaliland

Uganda

Kenya

0   500 km

Source B An Italian newspaper showing an Italian attack on soldiers in Abyssinia

In 1935 Italian troops invaded Abyssinia using tanks, poison gas, bombs and flame-throwers against Abyssinian troops armed with spears and out-dated rifles (Sources **B** and **C**). Haile Selassie appealed to the League for help. This presented Britain and France with a difficult problem.

Source C The Italian use of poison gas

WHEN KNIGHTS ARE BOLD.

"IT'S YOUR OWN FAULT. A CIVILISED MAN MUST PROTECT HIMSELF—AND WHAT'S MORE, IT'S BEGINNING TO RAIN."

The problem

As you study this problem take on the role of advising the British Government. You may remember that in 1935 Italy, Britain and France formed a group, 'the Stresa Front' to stand against the growing threat of Germany (page 45). The invasion of Abyssinia threatens to break up this group.

If Britain and France push the League to act against Italy then they could lose Italy as an ally and she might decide to ally with Germany. If the League does nothing then it is finished as a peace keeper. See if you can prevent this happening. First study Source **A**, then advise the British Government on which policy to support at the League. Follow the instructions to find out the results and consequences of your advice.

Choice of policies 1–5

1 Ignore the appeal for help from Haile Selassie (go to 7).
2 Condemn Italy, but do nothing else (go to 8).
3 Economic sanctions against Italy (go to 6).
4 Send troops (mostly British and French) to help Abyssinia (go to 13).
5 Suggest Abyssinia be divided, Italy to get the richer part, Abyssinia to keep the rest (go to 9).
6 This is a sound idea, now decide which sanctions:
   a) Everything, including materials needed for war such as oil and steel (go to 10).
   b) Everything as in **6 a)**, plus close the Suez Canal to Italian ships (go to 11).
   c) Only non essential items – as a warning to Italy (go to 12).

Results

7 You have failed straightaway. Even though Italy remains an ally, the League has failed. Read **C1** and try again.
8 This is a waste of breath. Mussolini ignores it. Read **C1** and try again.
9 When news of this leaks out it is so unpopular in Britain that you have to resign. Read **C1** and try again.
10 This should make Italy withdraw from Abyssinia provided other countries support sanctions. American and French oil companies oppose it, so toss a coin to see if sanctions succeed quickly (heads you win). Read **C3**.
11 This will quickly stop Italy as she cannot supply her army in Abyssinia. Read **C3**.
12 This fails to stop Italy, she wins the war before you can extend sanctions. Read **C1**.
13 The Italian Army is poorly equipped so you will probably succeed. Read **C2**.

Consequences

C1 This angers Abyssinia and other small nations in the League. The League has clearly failed, the idea of collective security is dead. Both Italy and Germany now believe they can get away with aggression.
C2 The League of Nations is at last seen to have teeth, this strengthens the League. Policies **3** and **6b** could have achieved the same result without the loss of life, other consequences are the same as **C3**.
C3 This is probably the best you can do. The League has succeeded but Italy is bitter, the Stresa Front breaks up, Italy leaves the League and looks to ally with Germany.

You can now see that it was impossible to save Abyssinia and keep Italy as an ally.

What actually happened?

The League agreed limited sanctions against Italy, but these did not include steel, oil or coal, which were vital to Italy. Britain and France did not close the Suez Canal. In December 1935 the British Foreign Secretary, Hoare, had secret talks with Laval, the Prime Minister of France, to allow Italy to keep the richer part of Abyssinia (Source **D**). But news of this was leaked, it was so unpopular that Hoare and Laval had to resign. By May 1936 Italy had won the war.

Source D A British cartoon criticising the Hoare-Laval Plan, 1935

THE SWEETS OF AGGRESSION.
Haile Selassie. "HAVE I GOT THIS RIGHT!—HE'S TAKEN NEARLY HALF OF WHAT I HAD. AND NOW YOU GENTLEMEN WANT TO DISCUSS WHETHER HE SHOULD TAKE ANY MORE!"

Source G AJP Taylor, *The Origins of the Second World War*, 1961

Source E In 1936 Haile Selassie again asked the League for help

I claim that justice which is due to my people and the assistance promised it eight months ago. That assistance has been constantly refused me. I assert that the problem submitted to the Assembly today is a much wider one than that of the situation created by Italy's aggression… It is the very existence of the League of Nations that is at stake.

Source F In May 1936 the Italians captured the capital of Abyssinia. Mussolini claimed a great victory.

Italy has her Empire – a Fascist Empire. An Empire of peace, because Italy desires peace, for herself and for all men, and she decides upon war only when it is forced upon her.

The consequences of failure

The League failed in Abyssinia. The consequences of this failure were very serious:

1 The League was now ignored as a peace keeping body (Source **G**).
2 It encouraged Mussolini to look for further military success and influence in the Mediterranean. He became involved in the Spanish Civil War which led to the fall of democracy in Spain and the rise of a Fascist dictator.
3 Italy's friendship with Britain and France suffered and the Stresa Front fell apart. Italy left the League.
   Mussolini moved closer to Hitler, first they pledged friendship in the Rome-Berlin Axis and followed it by Italy joining Germany and Japan in the Anti-Comintern Pact (an anti-Communist Pact).

The situation in Europe in 1936 was not promising. Although Russia had joined the League of Nations in 1934, Germany and Italy had left it. The League had failed to keep the peace by collective security.

The real death of the League was in December 1935. One day it was a powerful body imposing sanctions; the next day it was an empty sham, everyone scuttling from it as quickly as possible.

Questions

1 Which European power dominated this part of East Africa (see Source **A** on page 66)?

2 How did the Italian army attack the Abyssinian army? (See Sources **B** and **C**.)

3 Study Source **D**.
   a) Who do the characters in Source **D** represent?
   b) Why are Britain and France shown as policemen?
   c) How is the aggressor nation represented?

d) Why is Haile Selassie very angry? Is this anger justified?

4 Explain in your own words:
   a) Why the League failed in Abyssinia.
   b) Why this failure was so important.

5 What are the advantages and disadvantages for the historian of the following types of sources:
   a) other historians' accounts (e.g. Source **G**)?
   b) cartoons (e.g. Source **C**)?
   c) newspaper drawings (e.g. Source **B**)?

The League and disarmament

 Why did disarmament fail?

Disarmament

The other main aim of the League was to reduce armaments. But this was very difficult. It was not easy for countries to disarm after a long war, there was distrust between former enemies. France was particularly nervous because it had lost the safeguard of American support when the USA refused to join the League. French leaders believed they needed the security of a large army.

The main attempt at disarmament was the Disarmament Conference of 1932–34. Germany complained that she had been forced to disarm at Versailles and other countries should now do the same. This worried the French and they obstructed plans for reducing arms. Meanwhile, Germany was secretly rearming. In 1933 Germany withdrew from the Conference and the idea of disarmament was dead (Source **A**).

Source A The German Foreign Minister

The failure of the Conference was due solely to the unwillingness on the part of the highly-armed states to carry out their contractual duty to disarm.

1919	Universal disarmament proposed at the Paris Peace Conference
1921	Washington Naval Conference: Britain, USA and Japan agree not to build any new battleships or cruisers for ten years and to limit the size of their fleets
1925	Locarno Treaties cause hopes for disarmament to rise
1925–30	Most countries agree disarmament is desirable but no one wants to be first to disarm
1932	Disarmament Conference begins
1933	Germany withdraws from Conference and is already rearming
1934	Disarmament Conference ends in failure and most countries begin to rearm

Source B Timechart: Attempts at disarmament

Source C A British cartoon on the failure of the Disarmament Conference, 1933

Questions

1 Study Source **C**.
   a) What is breaking free?
   b) What point is the cartoonist making about disarmament?
   c) What does the reference to Professor Geneva mean?

2 Find evidence from page 35 to support the German claim in Source **A**.

The Failure of the League

▶ Why did the League fail?

Self-interest

The League did have some success. In the 1920s it helped settle some disputes. It also helped improve international communications, people's living and working conditions and joined the fight against slavery. But it failed in its main aim of preventing wars.

The Japanese invasion of Manchuria and the Italian invasion of Abyssinia were Problems 4 and 5 you considered on pages 50–51. Both were total failures for the League. Were you correct in your rating of the Leagues chances? Without American help the League had no real chance of stopping Japan, but Britain and France could have stopped Italy if they had acted quickly. The reason they did not act to stop the aggression is because they did not believe it was in their interest to do so and there was too much danger involved. Britain's self-interest is shown in Sources **A** and **B**.

Source A The British Prime Minister, Baldwin, to his friend Tom Jones, January 1936

I had in mind the menace of war; our fleet would be in real danger from the small craft of the Italians operating in a small sea. Italian bombers could get to London. I had also Germany in mind. Had we gone to war our anti-aircraft munitions would have been exhausted in a week. We have hardly got any armament firms left.

Source B A summary of a speech by Baldwin at a private dinner party in June 1936. Recalled by Harold Nicolson in his diary.

We knew that our great danger was not Italy, but Germany. We knew that if we crushed Italy we should not only destroy a possible ally, but weaken ourselves tremendously during the next two critical years, which are so dangerous.

Self-interest is one of several reasons why the League failed. The reasons are summarised opposite:

Source C A British cartoon drawn shortly after Italy's victory in Abyssinia, 1936

Reasons the League failed

	Reason	Consequence	Example
1	The USA did not join the League.	France felt insecure. The League had little power outside Europe. Weakened economic sanctions as a weapon.	No power to stop Japan, 1931.
2	Other important countries only belonged for brief periods.	Reduced the League's authority – it appeared as a European club led by Britain and France.	Russia joined 1934. Japan left 1931. Italy left 1937. Germany a member 1926–33.
3	The self-interest of leading members, especially Italy, Japan, Britain and France.	Aggression by Italy and Japan. Weak leadership by Britain and France.	Britain and France did not want to use economic sanctions against Japan, 1931.
4	Weapons: economic sanctions only ever used half-heartedly.	Gave an aggressor time to win.	1935–6 omission of oil, coal and steel from sanctions against Italy.
5	Weapons: the League never had its own army or asked members to provide troops.	Aggressors believed the League was toothless and not prepared to stand up to them.	Troops not used to stop Japan 1931 or Italy 1935.
6	Decisions needed to be unanimous and quick. This was difficult to achieve as meetings were few and far between.	One member in the Council could stop or delay a decision.	1931 – The Council voted 13 to 1 for Japan to leave Manchuria – the vote had no effect.
7	The Depression meant governments were more concerned with problems at home than problems in far away places.	Governments less likely to use economic sanctions as it might damage their trade.	Economic sanctions not used against Japan, only partly used against Italy.
8	The League was meant to uphold the Peace Treaties, but many countries came to believe that some of the terms were unfair and should be amended.	Some countries were not willing to act to enforce the Treaties, this weakened the League.	The German re-occupation of the Rhineland, 1936. The union of Germany and Austria 1938.
9	Responsibility for making the League work fell on Britain and France, but they did not trust each other and disagreed about problems.	Both were prepared to sign treaties outside of the League. The League lacked strong leadership.	The Anglo-German Naval Treaty, 1935. The Hoare-Laval Pact.

Questions

1 **a)** How do Baldwin's reasons in Source **A** differ from his reasons in Source **B**?
   b) Do the sources contradict each other? If so does this mean one is unreliable?

2 Does Source **B** help explain why Baldwin did not want to close the Suez Canal?

3 **a)** What can you see in the melting pot in Source **C**?
   b) Explain the title of the chef's recipe book.

4 The League has been described as 'a fragile life raft on the stormy seas of the 1930s'. Explain what this means and what caused the 'raft' to sink. Mention: aims; the Depression; disarmament; China; Abyssinia; self-interest.

7 Steps to war 1933–39

Step 1? 1933–35

▶ *What were Hitler's aims? How should other leaders react to Hitler?*

Hitler's aims

The Treaty of Versailles had tried to reduce and control Germany's strength. All German governments since 1919 wanted to reverse the Treaty. But in 1933 Germany had a new leader, Adolf Hitler, who was determined to destroy the Treaty, using force if necessary. This section looks at how far Hitler's Foreign policy led to the breakdown in international relations and the outbreak of the Second World War. This covers the years 1933–39. To help you understand the events you will be asked to advise the leaders of Britain and France, the two great democracies in Europe, on how to react to Hitler's actions. Your aim is to stop Hitler if you think he is wrong and to avoid war. When and how you do this is up to you – there was much disagreement on this at the time. Your teacher may give you a worksheet to help you organise your answers.

Before Hitler won power in Germany he made clear his aims in both his book, *Mein Kampf*, and his speeches. His aims were to:

1 Tear up the Treaty of Versailles;
2 Unite all Germans in a single Reich (Empire);
3 Win Lebensraum (living space) for Germans by invading the rich farmlands of Russia and Poland.

Each time you are asked to make a decision keep these aims in mind.

Rearmament

Hitler's first need was to rearm Germany but this was forbidden by the Treaty of Versailles. In 1933 Hitler pulled out of the Disarmament Conference. In May 1933 the British learnt that Germany was secretly rearming (Source **A**).

Source A A report to the British Cabinet

It is understood that there are at least 125 fighting aircraft in existence or being made... secret sources show that an order has been given by the German Government to the Dornier works for 36 twin-engined night bombers. The cost of these orders is to be disguised under funds for the employment of the unemployed. There are numerous indications in the last two months of increased activity in the German armaments industry.

Source B Bomb-aiming practice for the German airforce. The carpet simulates the land surface and the speed at which the aeroplane would fly.

Decision 1

Now advise Britain and France what to do by choosing one or more of the following policies. First think about the likely consequences of each piece of advice.

a) Accept Germany has a right to rearm as other countries are not disarming, and speed up your own rearmament.

b) Protest and try to persuade Germany to keep to the Treaty of Versailles.

c) Stop German rearmament – but you must also advise how to do it.

d) France should continue building a massive line of forts, the Maginot Line, along her border with Germany.

What is likely to happen if your advice is followed? Will Hitler be encouraged to continue to undo the Treaty of Versailles or will he be satisfied? Would your advice have been followed? Most British politicians accepted that the Treaty of Versailles needed to be changed and that Germany could partly rearm for her own security. The French did not agree, they wanted to keep Germany as a second rate power. But France was always reluctant to act without British support. Nothing was done to stop Germany rearming (Source **B**). By 1935 Germany's army had trebled to 300,000. Soon after, Hitler introduced conscription (Source **C**).

Austria, the Saar and the Stresa Front

Hitler believed all Germans should be united in a great German Empire. He was born in Austria and wanted Austria to be part of such an Empire. Some Austrians agreed with Hitler, others did not. The Treaty of Versailles forbade the union of Germany and Austria, but in 1934 Austrian Nazis murdered the Austrian leader and tried to take control. They hoped for support from Hitler, but the Italian leader, Mussolini, threatened to use force to stop Germany if she tried to invade Austria. Hitler was not ready for a war and backed down.

1935 was an important year for Hitler and things went well. Under the Treaty of Versailles the German industrial area called the Saar was due to vote on whether it wanted to return to German control. Ninety per cent voted in favour. This gave Hitler new large resources of coal, iron and steel.

The leaders of France, Britain and Italy were worried by the growing strength of Germany, so they agreed to stand together against Germany. But this agreement, known as the Stresa Front, soon fell apart. First Britain upset France by signing the Anglo-German Naval Treaty, this allowed Germany to build a navy up to 35% of the British fleet. Then, in 1936, Italy fell out with Britain and France when they opposed the Italian invasion of Abyssinia.

Source C Young Deutschland in chains… A German postcard issued shortly after Germany had introduced conscription.

Questions

1 What evidence in Source **A** shows that Germany was trying to keep their rearmament a secret?

2 a) Why do you think Source **C** was printed?
  b) Is the point made in the postcard a fair one?

3 Do you think any lessons were learned in 1934–35 by the leaders of either Germany, Britain, France or Italy?

4 Write the first entry in a report for the British Government dated 1935 explaining whether you think war is more likely, less likely or there has been no change in the situation. You will be asked to make further entries later on.

Step 2? The Rhineland 1936

 Should Britain and France act to stop Germany reoccupying the Rhineland? What were the consequences of the reoccupation?

March 1936

In March 1936 Hitler sent German troops into the Rhineland area of Germany. The Treaty of Versailles had demilitarised the area (no soldiers or weapons were allowed there). So Hitler had broken the Treaty of Versailles and the Locarno Treaties. (Sources **A** and **B**.) Should Britain and France act to stop Germany? They had to consider all the factors listed below. Study them carefully, you will be asked to make a decision.

Source A This British cartoon 'The March of Events' appeared two days after the reoccupation and shows Germany ignoring the diplomats who believe Germany will not reoccupy the Rhineland

Source B A German cartoon 'The New Germany buries the ghost of Versailles', 1936

Factors

Britain:

1 It was only 18 years since Britain had lost 5% of her active male population in the First World War.
2 British public opinion was against war and supported German control of the Rhineland (Source **C**).
3 Most politicians did not want to chance war (Source **C**).
4 Many people believed that German economic recovery was essential for Europe to recover.
5 The press opposed taking action.
6 Hitler promised peace (Source **C**).
7 The British Cabinet had decided in 1935 that the Rhineland was not vitally important.

France:

1 France had lost 10% of her male population in the war and public opinion was united that this must never happen again.
2 France had experienced 24 different governments in ten years and there was a general election in six weeks time.
3 There was no chance of help from the USA.
4 France had just ratified a defence pact with Russia.
5 French generals opposed acting alone against Germany.
6 The French army was inflexible, it was organized for defence not offence, it took a week to mobilise the army.
7 Of the 14,500 German troops sent to the Rhineland, only 3,000 were sent near the French border, the rest stayed near or behind

the Rhine (Source **D**). There were no tanks or bombers, and only ten armed aircraft.

8 French army leaders believed the German troops numbered 295,000.

9 Britain will only fight if Germany invades France.

Source C

A London taxi-driver commented to the British Foreign Secretary:

> I suppose Jerry (Germany) can do what he likes in his own back garden.

The British MP, Harold Nicolson, wrote in his diary:

> General mood of the House of Commons is one of fear. Anything to keep out of war.

Hitler promised in a speech in the Reichstag the day before reoccupation:

> We have no territorial demands to make in Europe… Germany will never break the peace.

Source D   The demilitarised area of the Rhineland, 1919–36

Key

The demilitarised area of the Rhineland 1919–1936

0   10 km

Decision 2

Hitler's actions were not a surprise, for several months the British had received reports of his plans to send in troops. Now advise the British and French Governments separately what to do. Remember your aim is to avoid war. Should they:

  a) Use force to remove the German army?
  b) Accept it and do nothing?

What might be the consequences of your advice this time – possibly one of the following?

1 German troops withdraw and Hitler's position as leader is weakened.

2 Hitler is a hero in Germany and is encouraged to believe France and Britain do not have the will to stop him tearing up the Treaty of Versailles.

3 Hitler will be satisfied and cause no more problems.

Are you happy your advice will help prevent war with Germany?

  Hitler believed he had taken a great gamble (Source **E**). His generals had advised against the gamble but Hitler had succeeded. Britain and France protested but did nothing more.

Source E   Hitler later explained

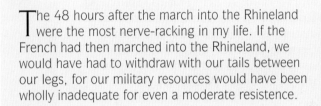

> The 48 hours after the march into the Rhineland were the most nerve-racking in my life. If the French had then marched into the Rhineland, we would have had to withdraw with our tails between our legs, for our military resources would have been wholly inadequate for even a moderate resistence.

The consequences

The consequences of Hitler's reoccupation of the Rhineland were important:

1 Germany built a line of forts along the Rhine. This protected the great industrial area of the Ruhr and made it more difficult to enter Germany to stop her breaking treaties.

2 France now had German troops right on her border.

3 Hitler was encouraged to take another gamble.

4 Britain and France began to rearm.

Questions

1 a) In Source **A** why do the diplomats believe Germany will not reoccupy the Rhineland?

  b) What is the German view of the Treaty of Versailles (the ghost) in Source **B**?

  c) Do Sources **A** and **B** agree in their views of the reoccupation?

2 Which factor supports Hitler's claim in Source **E**?

3 Which of the consequences do you think was the most important for the future of Europe? Why?

4 What was the key reason why **a)** Britain and **b)** France did not stop Hitler?

5 Make a second entry dated March 1936 in the report you began in Question 4 on page 73.

Step 3? Spain and Austria 1936–38

> *How did Hitler use the Spanish Civil War?*
> *How did Hitler achieve the union of Germany and Austria?*

Spain

In 1936 civil war began in Spain when the army and Fascist groups led by General Franco rebelled against the Republican Government. Europe seemed to be splitting into three opposing camps:

1 The democracies led by Britain and France.
2 The Fascist dictatorships of Germany and Italy.
3 Communist Russia.

Both Hitler and Mussolini sent troops and weapons to help Franco (Source **A**). Hitler hoped the war in Spain would distract Mussolini's attention from a German takeover of Austria. He also used the war to test German weapons, men and tactics (Source **B**).

This was the first time bombing had been used in Europe against civilians. This frightened the leaders of Britain and France. The British government calculated how many lives would be lost if London was attacked by bombers.

The Anti-Comintern Pact

A further warning sign came in November 1936 when Germany and Japan signed the Anti-Comintern Pact, this was an alliance against Communist Russia. In November 1937 Italy joined the Pact.

Austria

Hitler wanted the Anschluss – the union of Germany and Austria. In 1934 Mussolini had stopped Hitler invading Austria but now they were allies and the way was clear for Hitler to bully Austria into submission. First, Hitler ordered the Austrian Nazis to stir up trouble inside Austria.

Source A Civil War. Italian bombers destroy Republican planes at Liria, near Valencia.

Source B Noel Monks, an Australian journalist, described the town of Guernica shortly after it was bombed by the German Condor Legion in 1937

At 4 p.m. some 40 German and Italian aeroplanes came... By 7 p.m. there was no Guernica. About a thousand men, women and children lay in pieces among the market place, in the gutters and under the ruins where their homes had been... Friends picked up dud incendiary bombs branded with the German eagle.

Then, in February 1938, Hitler threatened the Austrian leader Kurt Schuschnigg to make him accept Nazis in his government (Source **C**).

Source C Schuschnigg later recalled Hitler's threats

I have only to give an order and in one single night all your ridiculous defences will be blown to bits... Don't think for one moment that anybody on earth is going to thwart my decisions. Italy? I see eye to eye with Mussolini... England? England will not move one finger for Austria... France? France could have stopped Germany in the Rhineland, but it is too late for France.

Schuschnigg ordered a vote on union with Germany. This angered Hitler and he threatened to invade. When there was no sign of support from Britain, France or Italy Schuschnigg gave way. In March Austrian Nazis took control and invited in German troops. Austria became part of Germany and Schuschnigg was sent to a concentration camp. Anschluss was forbidden by Versailles but Hitler had achieved it.

Decision 3

Can you save Austria? This is a very difficult problem, before you advise Britain and France consider these points:

1 The German army is now much stronger.
2 How would you get troops to Austria? They cannot go via Switzerland or Italy.
3 British rearmament will not be complete until 1939.
4 Most Austrians want Anschluss, but not all of them (Source **D**).

Think also about the consequences of your advice. Now decide, should Britain and France:

a) protest but do nothing else, or
b) enforce Versailles by sending troops?

Winston Churchill warned of the dangers of not acting (Source **E**).

Source E The warnings of Winston Churchill

Europe is confronted with a programme of aggression, there is only one choice open, either to submit like Austria, or else take effective measures while time remains to ward off the danger... Where are we going to be two years hence, when the German Army will certainly be much larger than the French Army, and when all the small nations will have fled from Geneva to make up to the ever growing power of the Nazi system?

Source D Austria, March 1938: Silent crowds watch the arrival of German troops at Innsbruck

The British Prime Minister in 1938 was Neville Chamberlain who was anxious to avoid war if possible. He believed some of Germany's demands were reasonable and that by agreeing to them war could be avoided and, if not, then at least it gave Britain time to rearm. This policy is called appeasement. Britain and France only protested over Austria.

Questions

1 Some historians argue that the Condor Legion did not destroy Guernica, but that the Republicans wrecked it for their own reasons. Do any of the sources contradict this view?

2 a) Why might a historian question the accuracy of Source **C**?
   b) What did Churchill mean in Source **E** when he said 'all the small nations will have fled from Geneva'?
   c) What can you learn from Source **D** about Austrians' views of the Anschluss?

3 Explain how between 1936–38 Mussolini became Hitler's ally (mention: Austria; Stresa Front; Abyssinia; Spain; Rome-Berlin Axis; Anti-Comintern Pact).

4 Make further entries dated November 1937 and March 1938 in your report on the likelihood of war.

Step 4? Czechoslovakia 1938

How did Czechoslovakia fall?

The Sudetenland

The union of Germany and Austria meant Hitler was well placed to achieve his next aim – the destruction of Czechoslovakia. It stood for what Hitler disliked most. It had been created by the Treaty of Versailles and was a successful democracy. It supported the League of Nations and was allied to Germany's enemies, France and Russia. Most of the population were Czechs and Slovaks who Hitler believed were inferior to the German 'master-race'. Also Czechoslovakia had defeated Germany 3–1 in the semi-finals of the 1934 football World Cup!

Hitler particularly wanted the Sudetenland area of Czechoslovakia where three million German speaking people lived (Source **A**). But Czechoslovakia was a much tougher nut to crack than Austria. It was protected by a strong line of forts and a modern army. It also had several allies.

First Hitler ordered the leader of the Sudeten Nazis, Konrad Henlein, to stir up trouble. Then Hitler claimed Sudetens were suffering at the hands of the Czechs. He threatened to invade to protect the Sudetens (Source **B**).

Source A   The break-up of Czechoslovakia

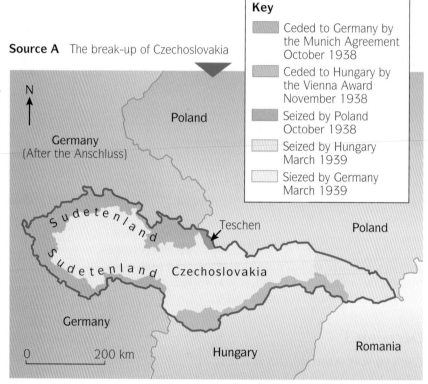

Key

- Ceded to Germany by the Munich Agreement October 1938
- Ceded to Hungary by the Vienna Award November 1938
- Seized by Poland October 1938
- Seized by Hungary March 1939
- Siezed by Germany March 1939

Source B   Hitler speaking to the German people, September 1938

The territory which belongs to Germany shall become German, and not after Benes (the Czech President) has succeeded in exterminating one or two million Germans, but now – immediately… It is the last territorial claim which I have to make in Europe… villages (in the Sudetenland) are burned down, attempts are made to smoke out the Germans with hand-grenades and gas… my patience is at an end. Benes will either give the Sudeten Germans their freedom, or we will go and fetch this freedom.

This would break the Treaty of Versailles. Also in 1925 France had promised Czechoslovakia military help if she was attacked by Germany. But France now had a different Government and the new leader, Daladier, was not keen on going to war to protect Czechoslovakia. The Czechs refused to be bullied and by September 1938 it seemed Europe would be dragged into war again.

Decision 4

Hitler is demanding the Sudetenland. Should Britain and France try to stop him? Before you give your advice study the following points:

1 Germany will be stronger if it controls the Czech armaments industry.
2 Czechoslovakia is a powerful ally to lose.
3 It appears Russia will help defend Czechoslovakia.
4 British rearmament is not complete, its army is still tiny.
5 Most British people support appeasement and believe Russia and Communism is a greater threat than Germany.

6 It is estimated that German bombs will kill 1.3 million Britons in the first 60 days of a war.

7 Hitler has said it is the last territorial claim he has.

Now advise Britain and France, should they:
  a) agree to Hitler's demands and desert the Czechs, or
  b) stand by Czechoslovakia.

Profile of Neville Chamberlain

Born in Britain in 1869, he became a successful business man.

In 1916 he was appointed director of National Service during the First World War and witnessed the horrors of war.

He became a Conservative MP in 1918 and in 1939 he became Prime Minister, His policy of appeasing Hitler was popular at first, at the same time he rearmed Britain. He resigned in May 1940 and was replaced by Winston Churchill as Prime Minister. In 1940 he died of cancer.

In a desperate bid to avoid war Chamberlain flew to Germany three times in September 1938 to talk to Hitler:

First visit 15 September at Berchtesgaden: Hitler insisted the Sudetenland become part of Germany. Chamberlain agreed. He then talked to France and Czechoslovakia. The French agreed but at first the Czechs did not. They only agreed when told Britain and France would not help if Germany attacked.

Second visit 22 September at Godesberg: Hitler did not want a peaceful settlement, so he was angry when Chamberlain returned to say the Czech had agreed. Hitler made new demands that Germany take the Sudetenland immediately and the claims of Poland and Hungary on parts of Czechoslovakia should also be met. Britain and France could not agree to this and began to prepare for war (Source **C**).

Source C Digging trenches in London, September 1938

Third visit   29 September at Munich: On the 28th Chamberlain was speaking to the House of Commons when news arrived that Hitler had agreed to a last minute conference on the Sudetenland crisis. MPs went wild with joy. So the next day the leaders of Germany, Britain, France and Italy (but not the Czechs!) met and agreed:

1 Germany could take the Sudetenland.
2 The claims of Poland and Hungary should be looked at.
3 Britain and France would protect what was left of Czechoslovakia.

Before Chamberlain left Munich he got Hitler to sign a declaration that both men would work for peace (Source **D**). On his return to Britain Chamberlain was given a hero's welcome (Source **E**). Most people believed he had kept the peace.

Source D   The declaration signed by Hitler and Chamberlain

We regard the Munich Agreement as a sign of the desire of our two people never to go to war with one another again.

Source E   Chamberlain on his return from Munich holding the agreement with Hitler which seemed to promise peace

Britain and France had deserted Czechoslovakia and given into Hitler's demands. The Czechs either had to accept the agreement or fight Germany, and probably Poland and Hungary as well. The Czechs agreed and on 1 October 1938 German troops marched into the Sudetenland.

After Munich Hitler continued much as before. Only six months later, in March 1939, German troops invaded most of the rest of Czechoslovakia. This gave Hitler control of the great Skoda arms factory and 2,200 artillery pieces, 600 tanks and 750 aircraft.

March 1939 – A turning point

The destruction of Czechoslovakia in March 1939 was a turning point in international relations in Europe. It was now clear that Hitler could not be trusted to keep any treaty or promise made to other countries. Fears for the future of Europe grew. People asked what Hitler would do next. Consider the following people and make the decision each is asked to make.

1 Britain: Susan Walker

Your father was killed in the last war. There is now talk of the government introducing conscription. You supported appeasement until now, but it has not stopped Hitler. Refer to page 37 and decide if either of the other two policies would have stopped Hitler.

2 France: Isabelle Dupont

You live in the village of Pozieres (see page 14). Your home was destroyed in 1915 and both your brothers killed. Only the river Rhine now separates France from the German Army. Study pages 34–35 and decide which reason for France's insecurity now worries you most.

3 Czechoslovakia: Paval Hasek

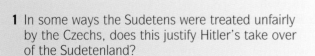

You now live under German control. Your street has been renamed Adolf Hitler Street. Until now you have driven on the left but now you are ordered to drive on the right as in Germany. Look back to pages 78–80, who do you blame for what has happened?

4 Poland: Anton Marchelowski

You fear both Germany and Russia. Hitler wants the return of land in Poland that once belonged to Germany. He is demanding the city of Danzig immediately. Stalin wants the land Poland won in the war of 1921. Read the first column on page 84 and decide if Russian troops should be allowed through Polish territory.

5 Russia: Ivan Asimov

Ivan is a corporal in the Soviet Army. Most of the officers have been purged by Stalin. As a good communist you hate Hitler and Nazism. Study 'The Nazi Soviet Pact' on page 85 and decide if Stalin is correct in deciding to sign a pact with Germany.

6 Italy: Maria Valenca

You are proud that other countries want to ally with Italy and that the Munich Conference was Mussolini's idea. In October 1936 Germany and Italy promised to help each other when they formed the Rome-Berlin Axis. Decide if Italy should fight alongside Germany if there is a war. Also decide if Mussolini should extend the Italian Empire by seizing Albania.

7 Germany: Peter Muller

You remember the last war and how Germany was humiliated afterwards at Versailles. You now have a job thanks to the Nazis and Germany is again a great power. Look back through 'Steps to War' (pages 72–80) and decide if Germany should continue to use aggression to retake land lost at Versailles.

8 USA: Jim O'Connor

You visited Europe once – as a soldier in 1917. As a good American you support democracy. Czechoslovakia was a democracy, but Europe is a long way away. Refer to pages 38–39 and decide if America was right not to join the League of Nations. Should America still avoid involvement in Europe?

Questions

1 In some ways the Sudetens were treated unfairly by the Czechs, does this justify Hitler's take over of the Sudetenland?

2 Do you think the people in Source **C** knew much about the Czechs?

3 Mussolini said 'Czechoslovakia was really Czecho-Germano-Polono-Magyaro-Rutheno-Roumano-Slovakia'. Czechoslovakia had been created in 1919 at Versailles.
   a) Use the map on page 78 to help explain what Mussolini meant and how this helped Hitler destroy Czechoslovakia.

   b) Does this mean the Treaty of Versailles was the reason why there was very nearly a war in Europe in 1938?

4 Are the following statements about Hitler supported by the evidence on pages 78–81?
   a) He was prepared to go to war in 1938.
   b) He was prepared to take chances.
   c) He misled other leaders.
   d) He was a clever politician.

5 Make further entries dated 28 September 1938 and 1 October 1938 in your report on the likelihood of war.

Appeasement 1938

▶ *Was appeasement sensible?*

Chamberlain's policy up until the Munich Agreement was called appeasement, he tried to satisfy Hitler's demands whilst rearming Britain in case force had to be used. In 1938 most people viewed appeasement as a success. After Hitler broke the Agreement in March 1939 most people saw it as a failure. Historians disagree on appeasement, many see it as a failure, but some have argued that at the time it was sensible and gave Britain time to prepare for war. Study these two different views of appeasement:

Appeasement was wrong because:

1 Hitler's aims were clear and he was fooling Chamberlain. This encouraged Hitler to think that Britain and France would not act to protect other countries.
2 Germany was not as strong as Britain thought she was, Germany was short of tanks, fuel and ammunition. Most German generals were worried by the prospect of war. It gave Hitler time to prepare for war.
3 The French army was still the stongest in Europe.
4 The Czechs had a modern well-equipped army and good defences.
5 The German airforce was not ready to launch a serious attack on Britain.
6 Russia appeared ready to help protect Czechoslovakia.
7 France's allies, Yugoslavia and Romania, lost confidence in France and tried to improve relations with Germany.
8 It was dishonourable to desert Czechoslovakia.

Appeasement was sensible because:

1 Germany's early demands, including the Sudetenland, were reasonable – they were simply about recovering German land and people lost at Versailles. Meeting these demands might satisfy Hitler.
2 German military superiority was never as great

THE GLUTTON

The glutton is a deep water fish with an elastic stomach, which enables it to swallow an indefinite amount of prey.

Source A A British cartoon 'The Glutton', Daily Herald, 17 March 1939

again as in September 1938. Britain only had a tiny land army in 1938. Military advisers encouraged Chamberlain to play for time to rearm, this was planned to peak in 1939–40.
3 The French army was organised only to defend France, not to help out Czechoslovakia.
4 The Czech army was divided, Slovaks and Sudeten Germans might not fight to protect Czechoslovakia. Czech defences were in the Sudetenland.
5 Britain was virtually defenceless against air attack in 1938.
6 Russia could not be relied on to help.
7 The most powerful countries in the British Empire were the self-governing dominions, Australia, Canada, South Africa and New Zealand. They made it clear they would not help Britain if she went to war over Czechoslovakia.
8 Britain was worried that Japan would threaten the Empire in the Far East. Britain was not strong enough to fight Germany and Japan at the same time.
9 The British public did not want to go to war over Czechoslovakia.

Many people, including Chamberlain, remembered the horrors of the last war and thought of the millions who would die in another war.

Do you think appeasement was sensible? Decide this by comparing the two sets of arguments. Do you think in 1938 'Britain should do the honourable thing and go to war to protect Czechoslovakia' or as Chamberlain thought 'The best policy is to hope for the best but be prepared for the worst'? Which points most influenced you in your choice?

Source B An American cartoon 'The Sign heard 'round the world', 29 September 1938

THE SIGH HEARD 'ROUND THE WORLD!

Interpretations

People interpret events and actions differently for several reasons, such as:

1 New evidence becomes available.
2 They want to promote their own beliefs.
3 They experience the consequences of events and actions and this affects their judgement.

Today, many historians are sympathetic to Chamberlain and point out that he favoured rearmament from early on and he hoped this would deter Hitler. Also, in February 1939 he agreed that Britain would help France defend itself and so committed Britain to sending a large army to fight on the continent. After Munich spending on rearmament increased rapidly, plans were made to evacuate children, and radar defences were rapidly improved. In September 1938 only the Thames estuary had radar, but by September 1939 there was a radar chain from the west of Scotland to the south coast of England.

Questions

1 Which of the reasons why interpretations differ might apply to views on Munich?

2 Do you think the account of events on these pages supports either of the interpretations?

3 Sources **A** and **B** show different views of appeasement at the time.

a) Explain which view they support.
b) They were drawn at different times, how might this explain their different views?

4 Explain why a policy of appeasement made sense to Chamberlain.

8 The final steps to war

The Nazi-Soviet Pact

 Why did Britain and France guarantee Poland's independence?
Why did Germany and Russia sign a non-aggression pact?
Why did Britain and France go to war?

Fear of Germany

Britain, France, Poland, Russia and Romania all feared Germany. Britain and France feared German domination of Europe. Poland feared German demands for the return of Danzig and the Polish corridor (Source **A**). Romania feared invasion because Germany wanted her oil fields. Russia was fighting Japanese attempts to take land in eastern Russia and feared war against Germany at the same time.

On 15 March 1939 German troops occupied what was left of Czechoslovakia. Hitler could no longer claim to be protecting Germans in a foreign country. It was now clear that he simply wanted to destroy Czechoslovakia and would break any treaty or agreement.

This caused a dramatic change in public opinion in Britain and France. The belief now grew that Hitler had to be stopped. This increased when Hitler's ally, Mussolini, demanded French territories in the Mediterranean. Also British rearmament was under way (Source **B**) and the French economy had rapidly improved. Together Britain and France decided on a tougher policy towards Hitler. They feared they might have to fight Germany, Italy and Japan at the same time. Chamberlain believed an alliance with Poland was the key. This would force Germany to fight a war on two fronts and Hitler feared this. Chamberlain wanted to join with France, Russia and Poland in a defensive alliance against Germany. But Poland feared Russia and would not let Russian troops enter Poland to counter a German attack.

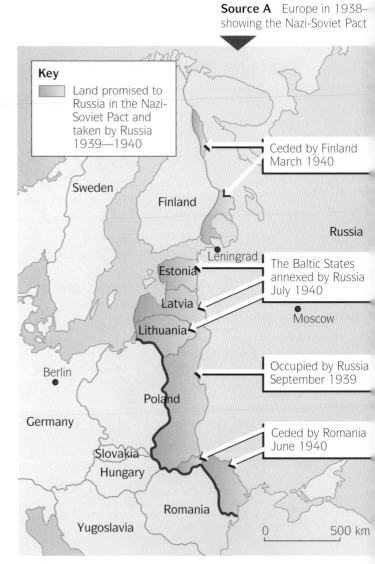

Source A Europe in 1938– showing the Nazi-Soviet Pact

Key
Land promised to Russia in the Nazi-Soviet Pact and taken by Russia 1939—1940

Sweden
Finland
Russia
Ceded by Finland March 1940
Leningrad
Estonia
The Baltic States annexed by Russia July 1940
Latvia
Lithuania
Moscow
Berlin
Occupied by Russia September 1939
Poland
Germany
Ceded by Romania June 1940
Slovakia
Hungary
Romania
Yugoslavia
0   500 km

Source B A British newspaper drawing from 1937 showing how the RAF was rearming as part of a five year plan

INCREASED DEVELOPMENT OF COASTAL DEFENCE SERVICES.
INCREASE IN RESERVES OF FUEL.
LARGE RESERVE OF STORES.
AIR-FORCE
BALLOON BARRAGES.
FURTHER INCREASE IN PERSONNEL.
75 NEW OPERATIONAL & TRAINING CENTRES & NUMEROUS NEW AERODROMES.
LARGE INCREASE IN MECHANICAL TRANSPORT.
FURTHER DEVELOPMENT IN LATEST TYPES OF AIRCRAFT.
G.H.DAVIS 1937.

As Poland would not co-operate with Russia, Britain believed she had to decide between an alliance with Poland or with Russia.

Decision 5

Advise Britain whether she should ally with Poland or Russia? The Soviet army is much larger but has a poor reputation and appears seriously weakened as Stalin has removed many of its officers. Poland defeated Russia in 1921, its army is of a reasonable size and Poland seems determined to stand up to Germany.

On 17 March there were strong rumours that Germany was about to seize Romania's oil fields. On 29 March a British journalist in Germany told Chamberlain and Halifax he was convinced Hitler was about to attack Poland unless it was made clear to Hitler that Britain would defend Poland. Chamberlain immediately decided on a guarantee to stand by Poland if she was invaded (Source **C**).

Source C   Lord Halifax, the British Foreign Secretary

In any scheme, the inclusion of Poland is vital as the one strong power bordering Germany in the East… We have to make a choice between Poland and Soviet Russia; it seems clear that Poland would give greater value.

The guarantee to Poland was announced on 31 March and changed the situation in Europe. It annoyed Stalin as Chamberlain had not consulted him. Stalin believed Chamberlain was trying to push Germany to attack Russia through the Baltic States without crossing Poland. It also annoyed Hitler who ordered his generals to prepare to invade Poland at the end of August.

The Nazi Soviet Pact

To help you understand what happened next it is best to look at events from the Russian point of view. See if you can spot seven reasons why Stalin signed a treaty with Hitler.

Events:
April: Russia suggests a treaty to Britain and France to help each other in the case of an attack. It is six weeks before Britain replies.
May–July: A Japanese army attacks positions on Russia's Far Eastern border. Stalin fears a war on two fronts, against Japan in the east and Germany in the west.
Early August: Negotiations begin between Russia and Britain and France, they are slow and complex. No senior people are sent to negotiate for Britain. Stalin concludes Britain and France are not serious. In truth Chamberlain is not keen on an alliance with Russia. Stalin is also talking to Germany about a treaty.
20 August: Russia and Japan are involved in the Battle of Nomonhan. This fierce battle rages for 11 days.
20 August: Hitler writes to Stalin offering talks with his foreign minister, Ribbentrop.
21 August: Talks with Britain and France break down as Poland will not let Russian troops cross Poland.
23 August: Ribbentrop flies to Russia. He tells Stalin war with Poland is imminent and offers Stalin a non-aggression pact and control of parts of Eastern Europe. Stalin was now faced with a choice:
Choice one: to avoid war by a pact with Germany in which they promise not to attack each other. A secret clause promised Russia parts of Poland and Romania, and control over Lithuania, Estonia, Latvia and Finland.
Choice two: to chance war by signing a military alliance with Britain and France. This offered no land and meant Russia would do most of the fighting. Britain did not yet have a large army ready to fight and the French army was prepared only for defence. Although Russia was winning the conflict with Japan, Stalin played safe and signed a non-aggression pact with Germany on 23 August (Source **D**).

Source D   A British cartoon from December 1939 commenting on the new friendship between Russia and Germany

85

Germany invades Poland

The Nazi-Soviet Pact was decisive as it meant Poland could not be defended. Hitler knew this, when he heard it had been signed he banged the table in delight and shouted, 'I have them'.

Chamberlain told Hitler again that Britain and France would fight for Poland. Hitler learnt that Italy and Japan, annoyed by his pact with Russia, would remain neutral. He postponed the invasion for a few days and offered Britain a deal. If Germany was allowed to invade Poland, Hitler would guarantee to leave the British Empire alone (Source **E**).

'We offer you quiet, repose and everlasting PEACE!'

Putting the Lid on It!

Source E Hitler and Stalin make an offer to Britain and France

Source F Results from opinion polls in Britain and France

British result

October 1938: In the present situation do you favour increased expenditure on armaments?

Yes	72 %
No	18 %
No opinion	10 %

December 1938: If there is a war between Germany and Russia, which side would you rather see win?

Germany	15%
Russia	85 %

March 1939: Would you like to see Great Britain and Soviet Russia being more friendly to each other?

Yes	84 %
No	7 %
No opinion	9 %

April 1939: Is the British Government right in following a policy of giving military guarantees to preserve the independence of small European nations?

Yes	83 %
No	17 %

French result

October 1938: Do you think that Britain and France should resist any further demands by Hitler?

Yes	70 %
No	17 %
No opinion	13 %

June 1939: Do you think that, if the Germans try to seize Danzig (in Poland), we should stop them by force?

Yes	76%
No	17 %
No opinion	7 %

Decision 6

This is your final decision. Before you give your advice study Source **F** to see if the public in Britain and France believe Germany should now be stopped. The countries and dominions of the British Empire will now support Britain in a war against Germany.

Poland refused to give in to Hitler's bullying (Source **G**). On 1 September German troops invaded Poland. On 3 September Britain and France declared war on Germany. Was your advice followed? Hitler was surprised but not worried (Source **H**).

Now advise Britain and France whether they should accept Hitler's offer or declare war on Germany if she invades Poland.

Source G A Polish newspaper declared:

The whole people will fight with determination for Polish freedom and independence. Nothing will be given up without a fight. Every Polish house will be a fortress which the enemy will have to take by storm. The danger from the air will not daunt Poland… Whoever seeks a quarrel with Poland will have more to lose than to gain.

Source H Hitler had boasted on 22 August

I experienced those poor worms Daladier and Chamberlain in Munich. They will be too cowardly to attack. They won't go beyond a blockade. Against that we have self sufficiency and the Russian raw materials. Poland will be depopulated and settled with Germans… After Stalin's death – he is a very sick man – we will break the Soviet Union.

Europe was at war again only twenty years after the last war. All the attempts at keeping the peace had failed.

One of the reasons for studying History is to avoid making the same mistakes again. You might think that the same mistakes led to war in both 1914 and 1939, or you might think that the causes of war in 1914 were different from the causes of the Second World War. Look back to pages 10–11 and compare the causes of the two wars.

Source I asks why the lessons of History have not been learnt. The character 'History' leans on the blood stained book 'History of Humanity' in despair. He does not blame any particular country or individual, the responsibility is universal.

At the time most people on the side of the Allies blamed Hitler for causing the war. Other people also blamed one or more of the other men involved in international relations between the wars: Clemenceau, Wilson, Lloyd George, Chamberlain or Stalin.

On the next page you will consider some of the different interpretations of the causes of war in 1939.

Source I Lessons of History. An American cartoon 4 September 1939.

1 Why do you think Source **B** on page 84 was printed by the newspaper?

2 **a)** What does the cartoonist, David Low, think of the Nazi-Soviet Pact (see Source **D** on page 85)?
   b) David Low's cartoons were banned in Germany. Why do you think Hitler did this?

3 What does the cartoonist in Source **E** think of the offer?

4 Study Source **F**.
   a) Was Chamberlain's view of Russia similar to that held by the British public?
   b) Which opinion poll suggests the British public supported the guarantee to Poland?

   c) Was the view of Germany held by the public in Britain and France similar?
   d) Do the opinion polls in France show a hardening of opinion against Germany?
   e) Opinion polls were just beginning at this time, what determined how accurate they were?

5 Explain why Britain and France went to war with Germany in September 1939. In you answer mention: the Rhineland, Munich, rearmament.

6 Why did Hitler think Britain and France would not fight to save Poland? In your answer you could mention: the Rhineland, appeasement, the Nazi-Soviet Pact.

The causes of war – Interpretations

▶ **Why did war break out in Europe in 1939?**
Do historians agree?

Why did war break out in Europe? Was the main reason the Peace Treaties after the First World war, or Hitler, or the policy of appeasement, or was it all of these? On a copy of Source **A** work out how the various causes of war contributed to the outbreak of war.

Source A

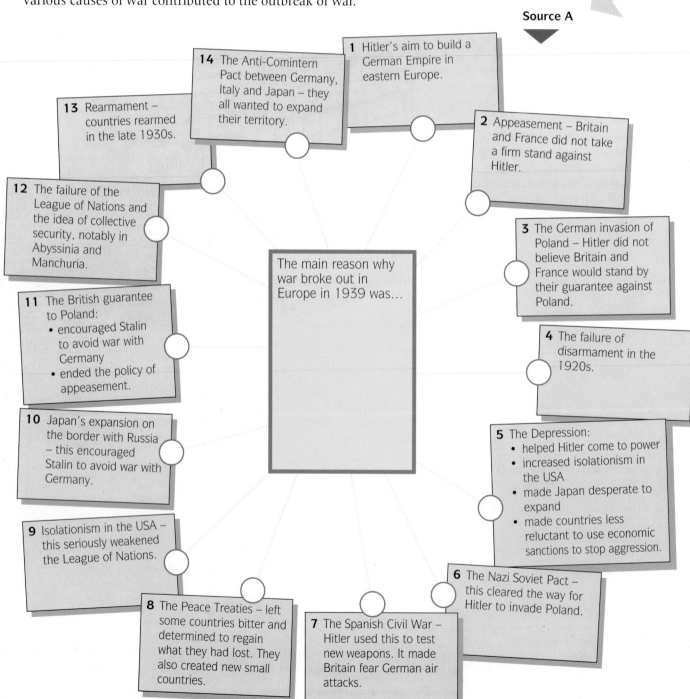

1 Hitler's aim to build a German Empire in eastern Europe.

2 Appeasement – Britain and France did not take a firm stand against Hitler.

3 The German invasion of Poland – Hitler did not believe Britain and France would stand by their guarantee against Poland.

4 The failure of disarmament in the 1920s.

5 The Depression:
• helped Hitler come to power
• increased isolationism in the USA
• made Japan desperate to expand
• made countries less reluctant to use economic sanctions to stop aggression.

6 The Nazi Soviet Pact – this cleared the way for Hitler to invade Poland.

7 The Spanish Civil War – Hitler used this to test new weapons. It made Britain fear German air attacks.

8 The Peace Treaties – left some countries bitter and determined to regain what they had lost. They also created new small countries.

9 Isolationism in the USA – this seriously weakened the League of Nations.

10 Japan's expansion on the border with Russia – this encouraged Stalin to avoid war with Germany.

11 The British guarantee to Poland:
• encouraged Stalin to avoid war with Germany
• ended the policy of appeasement.

12 The failure of the League of Nations and the idea of collective security, notably in Abyssinia and Manchuria.

13 Rearmament – countries rearmed in the late 1930s.

14 The Anti-Comintern Pact between Germany, Italy and Japan – they all wanted to expand their territory.

The main reason why war broke out in Europe in 1939 was…

Historians do not agree on why war broke out. In particular they disagree on whether Hitler planned the war and how far he was to blame. Below are three interpretations. Which of these is most similar to the interpretation you arrived at in Source **A**?

Interpretation one – The First World War and the Peace Treaties

The Treaty of Versailles had punished Germany very harshly. Many Germans found themselves living in other countries such as Poland. Therefore, many Germans were happy to listen to anyone who promised to regain what Germany had lost. In the 1930s the Depression made life in Germany very difficult. Germany was still paying reparations demanded at Versailles. The one person who seemed to offer hope was Hitler. He restored the economy and German pride, and recovered German territory. Germany was recovering her strength but Britain and France were afraid of this and decided to stop Germany.

Interpretation two – Opportunities, miscalculations and appeasement

In 1961 the historian AJP Taylor published a book *The Origins of the Second World War*. He argued that Hitler had no plan but simply took opportunities as they arose to undo the injustice of Versailles. Britain, France, Russia and the USA (the Allies) could not agree on how to deal with Hitler. When war came it was a miscalculation by Hitler, he did not expect Britain and France to go to war over Poland. The policy of appeasement had encouraged him to believe Britain and France would give way rather than fight. If the Allies had stood up to Hitler earlier he would have backed down and war would have been avoided.

Interpretation three – Hitler

The historian Allan Bullock argues that Hitler was the cause. In *Mein Kampf* Hitler had set out his plan to create a racial state and conquer large areas of eastern Europe. Hitler took over Austria, Czechoslovakia, and Poland. He was following his plan and he knew a war would be necessary. Although other factors contributed to war, the main cause was Hitler.

Source B This British cartoon appeared in April 1939

Questions

1 Why would historians during and immediately after the war agree that the cause of war was the aggression of Hitler?

2 Why might historians such as AJP Taylor later come to a different interpretation?

3 Who do you think Russian historians blamed for the war?

4 Which interpretation would the cartoonist who drew Source **B** be most likely to agree with?

9 The world at war 1937–41

Japan invades China 1937–39

▶ **Why did Japan invade China? What did other powers do to stop Japan?**

Invasion

Today the Japanese call the years 1931–41 the Kurai tanima (dark valley). It was a time when the army had a great deal of power. Japan's success in Manchuria in 1931 strengthened the power of the army, and of those politicians who wanted to expand the Japanese Empire. Japan believed she had to expand to survive. She had lost many of her overseas markets in the Depression and had other problems such as over-population, land shortage, and a need for raw materials such as oil and coal. Therefore, Japan decided to invade more of China.

In July 1937 Japanese troops clashed with Chinese troops at Marco Polo Bridge, south of Beijing. The Japanese said the fighting started accidentally – because the Japanese commander thought one of his men had been captured by the Chinese, but he had only been relieving himself in nearby bushes. The Japanese had carefully planned the incident to give them an excuse to invade the rest of China. They soon captured most of north-east China and Shanghai (Source **A**).

Source A A British journalist visited Shanghai after the attack

There is hardly a building standing which has not been gutted by fire. Smouldering ruins and deserted streets… The only living creatures being dogs unnaturally fattened by feasting on corpses. Of a population of about 100,000 I saw only five Chinese.

The Japanese soldiers took a delight in killing. They even made it a competition (Sources **B** and **C**).

Source B A Japanese newspaper reported

SUB-LIEUTENANTS IN RACE TO FELL 100 CHINESE RUNNING CLOSE CONTEST
Sub-Lieutenants Mukai and Noda in a friendly contest to see which of them will first fell 100 Chinese in individual sword combat… are running almost neck to neck. On Sunday the 'score' was Mukai 89, Noda 78.

Source C China, the battle of Shanghai

Source D A British cartoon from 1937 showing the reluctance of Britain and America to interfere in the Japanese invasion of China

"S-S-SHOULDN'T WE DO SOMETHING?"
"T-TOO RISKY! L-LET'S STAY HERE AND DEPLORE."

MASS MURDER IN CHINA.

A week later the newspaper explained that the target was now 150 killings:

> **MUKAI'S BLADE WAS SLIGHTLY DAMAGED**
> He explained that this was the result of cutting a Chinese in half, helmet and all. The contest was 'fun' he declared.

In December 1937 Nanjing was captured. The Japanese committed terrible atrocities in the city, raping, murdering and torturing thousands of people.

The League and Japan

China appealed to the League of Nations, but by 1937 it was powerless. It condemned Japan but did nothing else, Japan had left the League in 1932. The idea of collective security had died in the mid-1930s. Britain and France even continued to sell war materials to Japan. The USA was unwilling to take any action that might endanger her trade with Japan (Source **D**). Japan ignored the League and continued to push forward. Millions of Chinese retreated west.

'A New Order in East Asia'

By the end of 1938 the Japanese had invaded most of eastern China (Source **E**). They controlled the towns and cities but not the countryside where Chinese soldiers were in control. In November 1938 Japan announced a 'New Order in East Asia'. The idea was that Japan, Manchuria and China would unite under the leadership of Japan. This was the first step towards establishing a 'Greater East Asia Co-prosperity Sphere', an area controlled by Japan which was self-sufficient and free from Western control.

Source E David Bergamini, a child of ten at the time, later recalled:

> Through our field glasses I looked into the front lines of Japanese occupied China. Japanese soldiers were conducting a reprisal raid against a Chinese farm village, bayoneting its inhabitants and systematically burning its huts… They took food from the starving, raped little girls, cut open pregnant women, threw infants into the air and caught them on bayonets.

Questions

1 How does Source **B** support the description in Source **E** of how the Japanese treated their enemies?

2 Study Source **D**.
  a) Does the cartoonist think Britain and the USA had the power to try to stop Japan?

  b) What is the cartoonist's view of the actions of Britain and the USA?

3 Why was Japan so aggressive towards her neighbours?

The spread of war 1939–41

 Why did the USA end her isolation? Why did Japan attack the USA?

The USA and Europe

In 1919 the USA had adopted a policy of isolating itself from quarrels in Europe. In 1933 Franklin D. Roosevelt became President. He accepted that Americans wanted to keep out of war (Source **A**) and in 1935 and 1937 neutrality laws were passed. If war broke out then the USA could not trade with or lend money to those involved.

Source A From a speech by F.D. Roosevelt, 1936

I have seen war. I have seen blood running from the wounded. I have seen men coughing out their gassed lungs. I have seen the dead in the mud. I have seen cities destroyed… I have seen children starving. I have seen the agony of mothers and wives. I hate war.

But as Europe drifted to war in 1939 Roosevelt began to believe that America could not just stand and watch. Democracy was under threat from Hitler. Roosevelt warned that if the Axis powers (Germany and Italy) conquered Europe, then Africa would be next and then Central and South America would be threatened.

Source B A British view of Lend-lease

The Lend-lease Plan

When war broke out in Europe American opinion began to change. Roosevelt began to work closely with the new British Prime Minster, Winston Churchill. The American Congress changed the law so that arms could be sold to Britain and France. Then in March 1941 the Lend-lease Plan was passed which allowed America to 'lend' Britain vital war materials, including warships, tanks, planes and food (Source **B**). Roosevelt compared it to lending a garden hose to help a neighbour put out a fire. One of his opponents said it was more like lending chewing gum – 'You don't want it back again'.

World War

In 1941 the war spread beyond Europe. In North Africa, Ethiopia, Kenya and the Sudan fierce fighting took place between British and Commonwealth forces on one side and German and Italian forces on the other.

The next step to world war came in June 1941 when Hitler ignored his non-aggression pact with Stalin and launched 'Operation Barbarossa', the invasion of Soviet Russia. Hitler saw Russia as providing food and slave labour for his 'master race'. Germany was helped by Finland, Romania, Hungary and Slovakia. They captured a huge area of western Russia. America extended Lend-lease help to Russia.

Japan's rivalry with the USA

Japan refused to join the attack on Russia. A Japanese army had been defeated at the Battle of Nomonhan in 1939 and in 1941 the two countries had signed a non-aggression pact. Japan now looked south to expand her empire. She wanted to create a 'co-prosperity sphere' from the influence of white people (Source C). She knew this would bring her into conflict with the USA and Britain.

Source C A Japanese army officer

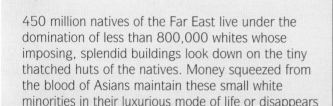

450 million natives of the Far East live under the domination of less than 800,000 whites whose imposing, splendid buildings look down on the tiny thatched huts of the natives. Money squeezed from the blood of Asians maintain these small white minorities in their luxurious mode of life or disappears to the home counties. Is this really God's will?

The USA was the only nation with the power to stop Japan in East Asia. America had considerable amounts of money invested in the area and became worried about the growing power of Japan's army and navy. The USA tried to warn off Japan by increasing the size of the American navy in the Pacific, giving more aid to China and refusing to trade certain goods with Japan.

When France fell to Germany in 1940 the Japanese took the opportunity to extend their empire by invading French-Indo China (Source **D**). This led the USA, Britain and the Netherlands to stop the sale of oil to Japan. Foreign oil was essential to Japan as she only produced 10 % of the oil she needed. Japan felt under siege and some leaders argued the only solution was to go to war to seize the oil fields in the Dutch East Indies.

In September 1940 Japan entered an alliance with Germany and Italy. Relations between Japan and America became worse in 1941. The USA demanded that Japan withdraw from China and ordered a 'freeze' on Japanese money and property in the USA. But Japan could not face such a loss of markets and raw materials. The economic sanctions were hurting her.

In October 1941 General Tojo became Prime Minister of Japan. His nickname was 'The Razor' because he believed in using the army to achieve Japan's aims. He would not accept America's demands.

Source D Japanese expansion to 1941

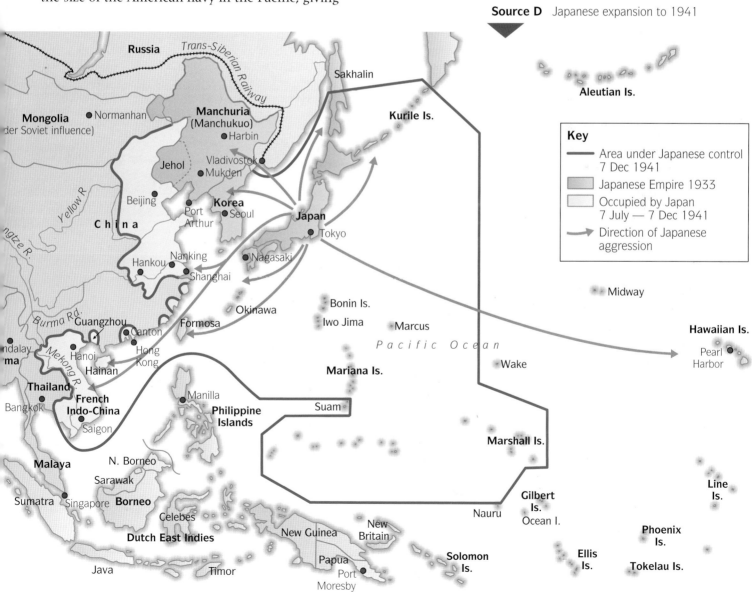

Pearl Harbor 1941

General Tojo believed Japan had no alternative but to fight, but Japan's leaders were not sure they could win a war against the USA. If Japan could knockout the American Pacific fleet then Japan could strengthen herself by building her empire before America had recovered. So, without warning in 1941, on 7 December, 350 Japanese aircraft attacked the American naval base at Pearl Harbor (Sources **E** and **F**). Some 18 American warships were damaged or sunk, 87 aircraft destroyed and over 2,400 people killed. On 8 December America declared war on Japan. The same day Japan attacked Malaya and the Philippines. Three days later Germany and Italy declared war on the USA. The world was now at war.

Source E   Major General H.C.Davidson

We did not have the guns loaded. That was our greatest difficulty… Especially since the hangers where we had the ammunition stored were on fire, and the ammunition was afire too.

Source F   American warships under attack at Pearl Harbor

Source G   The leaders of the Allies in 1943: Stalin, Roosevelt and Churchill

Profile: Franklin D. Roosevelt

Born in 1882 into a rich family. He qualified as a lawyer and entered politics as a Democratic senator in 1910.

In 1921 he was partly paralysed by polio. This experience gave him a deep compassion for human suffering.

Elected President in 1933. He believed in the 'American Dream' that anyone who worked hard could become rich.

To pull America out of the Depression he began the 'New Deal', a massive programme of work and benefits for the unemployed. This made him very popular and he was elected President four times.

He formed a close friendship with Winston Churchill and became convinced the USA should enter the war.

Died in 1945.

Profile of Winston Churchill

Born in 1874 into a rich aristocratic family.

Joined the army and fought in North Africa. He became a journalist and reported on the Boer War in South Africa. He was captured by the Boers, escaped and returned to England as a hero.

Became an MP in 1900. He served in the National Government during the First World War.

Opposed Chamberlain's policy of appeasement.

In 1937 he became First Lord of the Admiralty and in 1940 Prime Minister. He led Britain through the war and proved a great leader.

In 1945 he was defeated in the election, but was Prime Minister again between 1951–55.

He retired from politics in 1955 and died in 1965.

Questions

1 Study Source **B** on page 92.
  a) Why has the cartoonist used the description 'Happy Event'?
  b) Who would be likely to disagree with this view?

2 **a)** Does Source **C** provide Japan with a valid reason for her aggression in East Asia?
  b) In their own war games before Pearl Harbor the Japanese usually lost to the USA. So why did they start a war with the USA?

3 **a)** Do you think Roosevelt was speaking the truth in Source **A** on page 92?
  b) Explain why, after 1939, Roosevelt gradually ended America's policy of isolation?
  c) What feelings were Americans likely to have on hearing the news of Pearl Harbor?
  d) Were the Americans at Pearl Harbor prepared for an attack?

4 All of the following were reasons for the Japanese attack on Pearl Harbor:
  i) Japan's desire to build an empire;
  ii) The effect of the Depression on Japan's economy;
  iii) America's refusal to sell oil to Japan;
  iv) General Tojo became Prime Minister in October 1941;
  v) The wish to remove European influence in East Asia.
  Were all these reasons equally important, refer to each in your answer.

5 In what ways were the causes of war in the Pacific both similar and different to the causes of war in Europe?

6 The war was going badly for Britain and her allies in 1941, but when Churchill heard the news of Pearl Harbor he said, 'I went to bed and slept the sleep of the saved and thankful'. What do you think he meant?

Index